SUGAR SKULL COLORING BOOK
Volume 4

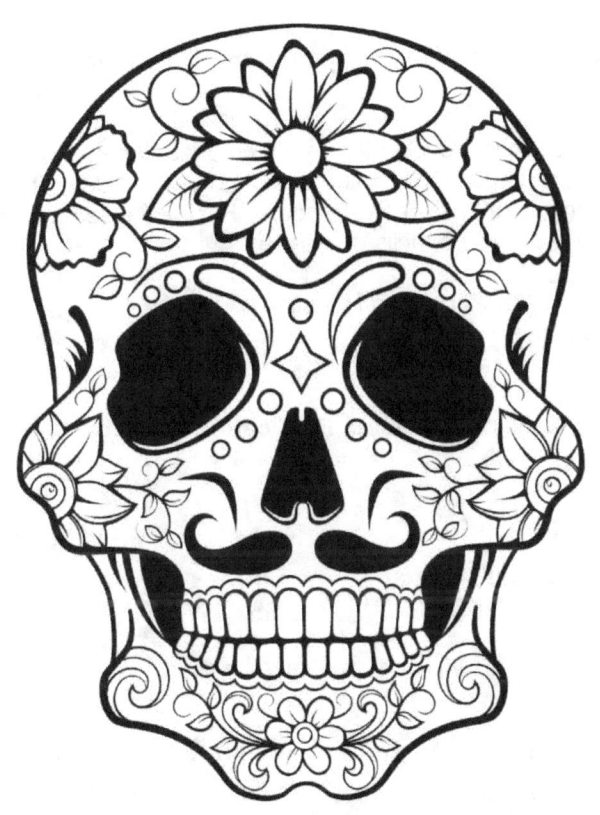

Dr. Melissa Caudle

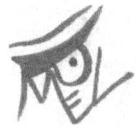

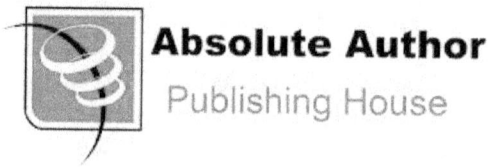

www.AbsoluteAuthorPublishingHouse.com

Sugar Skull Coloring Book Volume 3
Copyright © 2022 by Dr. Melissa Caudle
All Rights Reserved

No drawing can be copied, printed, or reproduced in any form without the written consent of Dr. Melissa Caudle.

Coloring Hints: It is strongly advised that each colorist place a piece of cardstock or file folder behind each page as you color to avoid bleed through. This is especially important when using markers or watercolor. For two-side coloring books, I recommend only using colored pencils or crayons.

Publisher: Absolute Author Publishing House
Editor: Dr. Carol Michaels
Cover Designer: Dr. Melissa Caudle

Library of Congress Catalogue In-Data Publication

p. cm.

Hardback ISBN: 978-1-64953-613-6
Paberback ISBN: 978-1-64953-615-0

About the Author

Dr. Melissa Caudle is an award-winning screenwriter, illustrator, and bestselling author of over 100 books for adults and children.

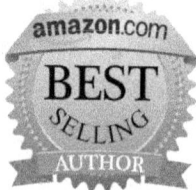

PRINTED IN THE UNITED STATES OF AMERICA

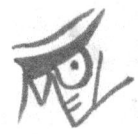

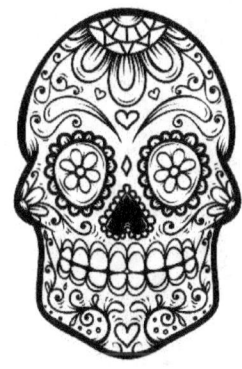

THIS BOOK BELONGS TO

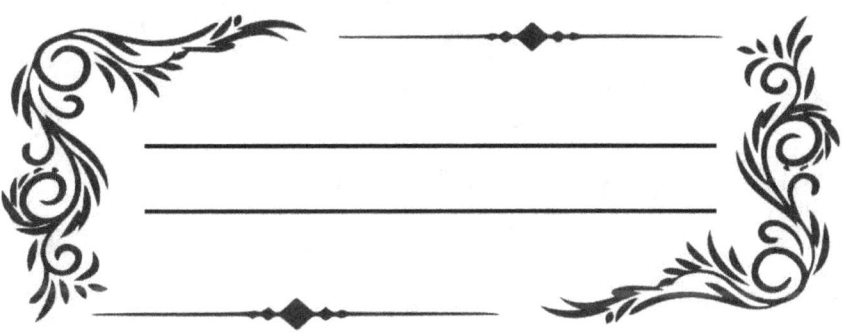

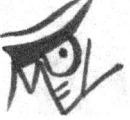

COLOR TEST PAGES

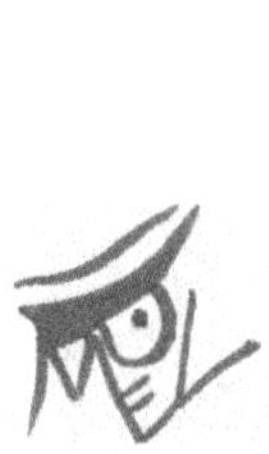

COLOR TEST PAGES

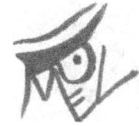

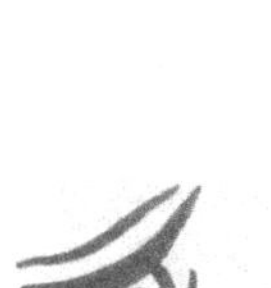

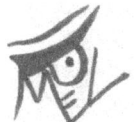

COLOR TEST PAGES

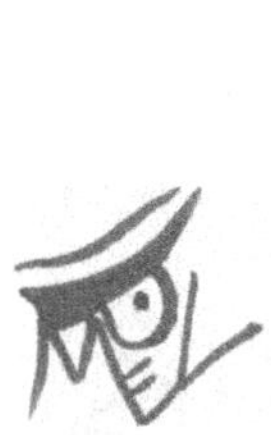

COLOR TEST PAGES

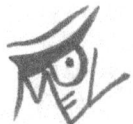

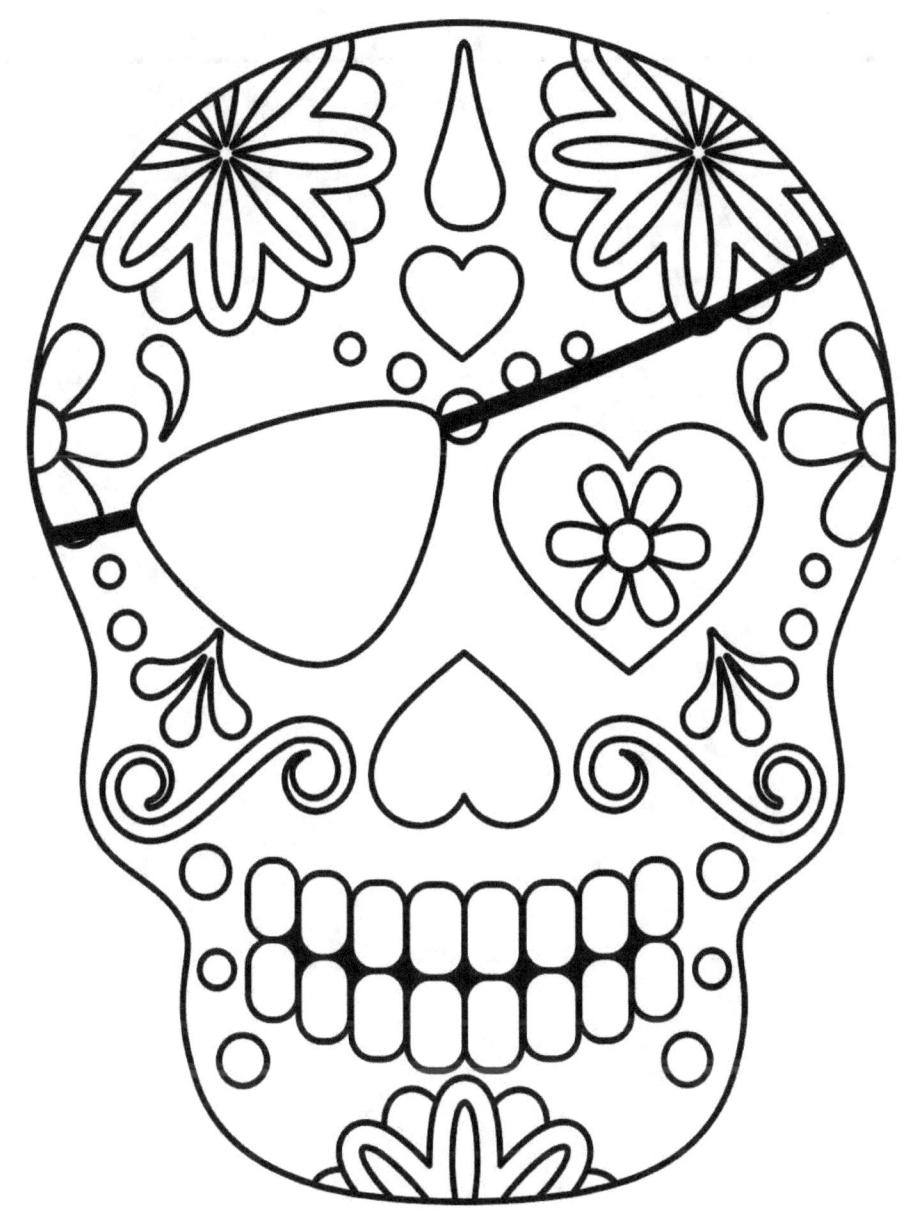

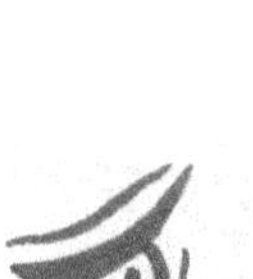

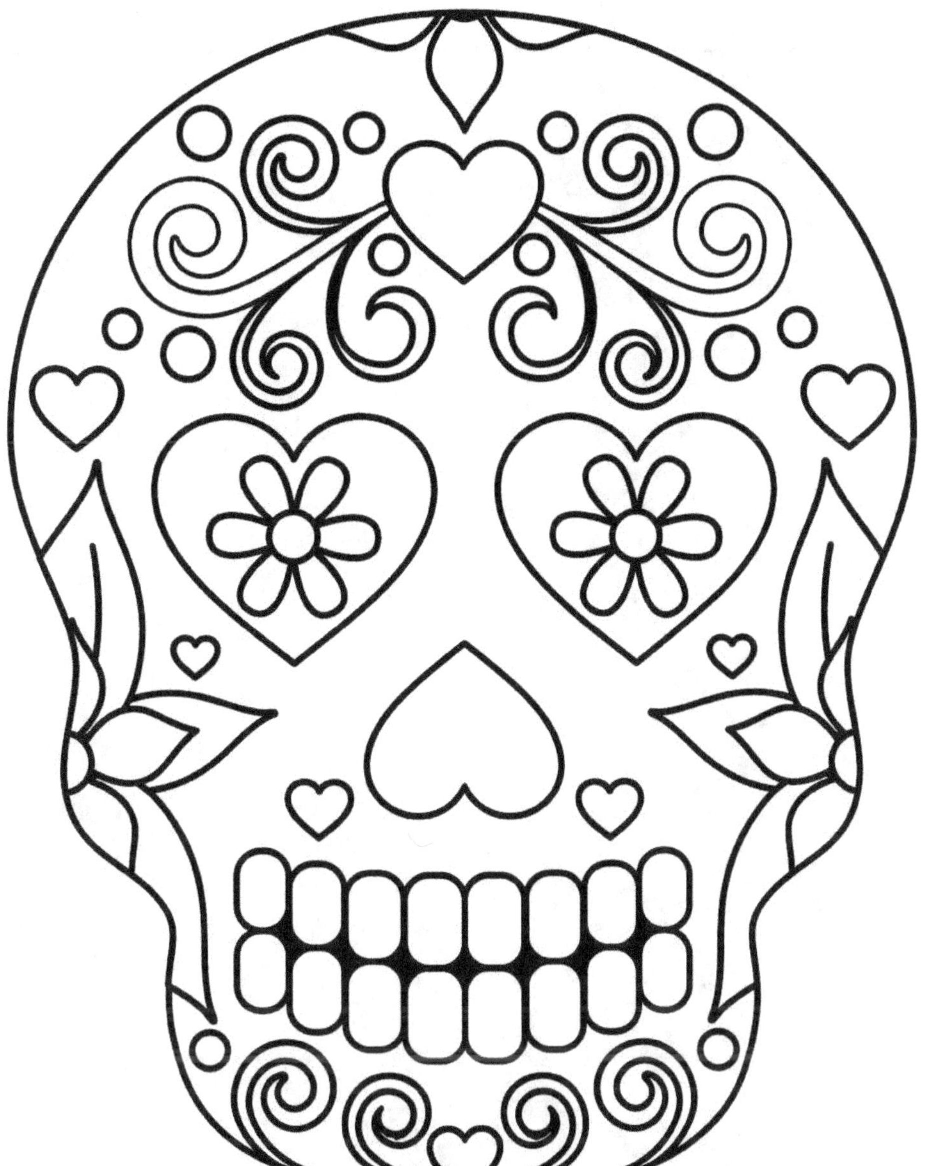

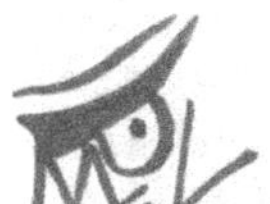

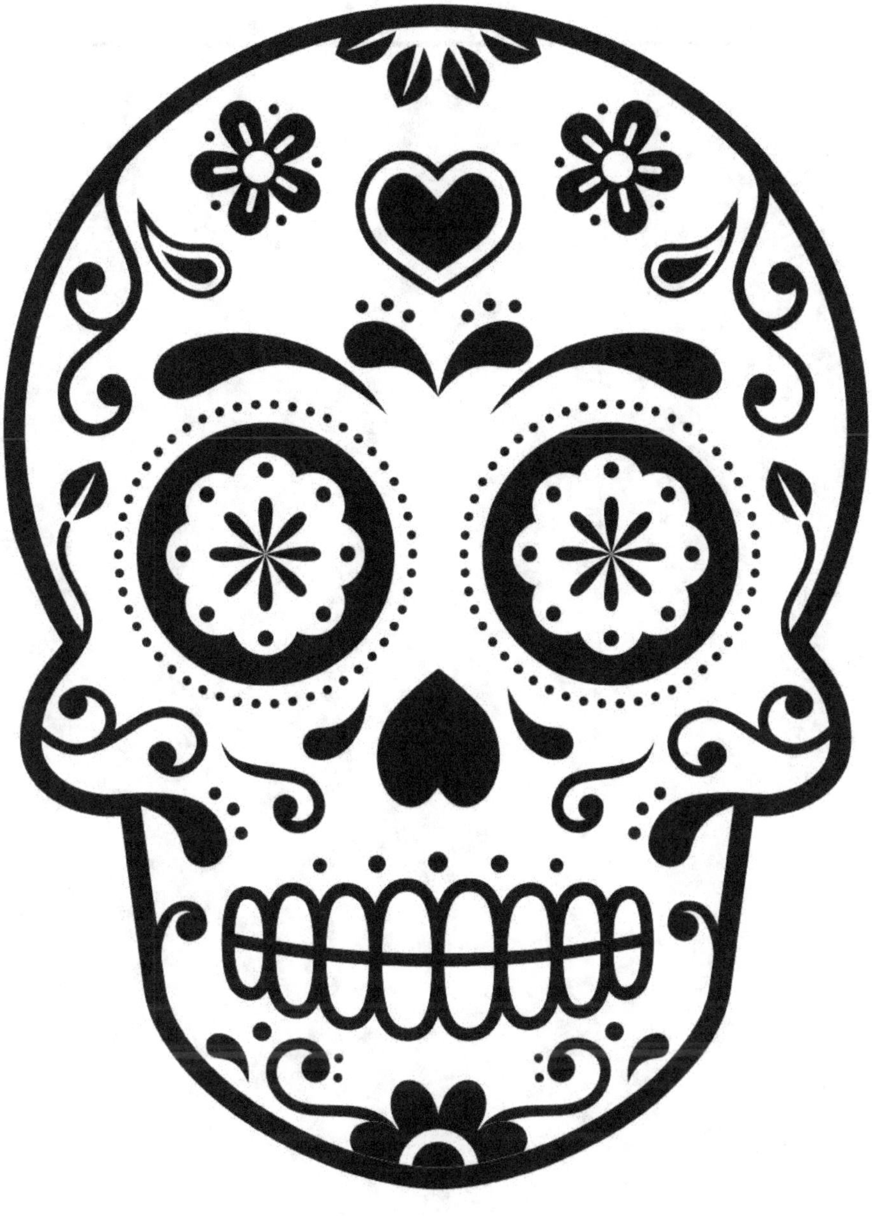

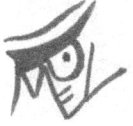

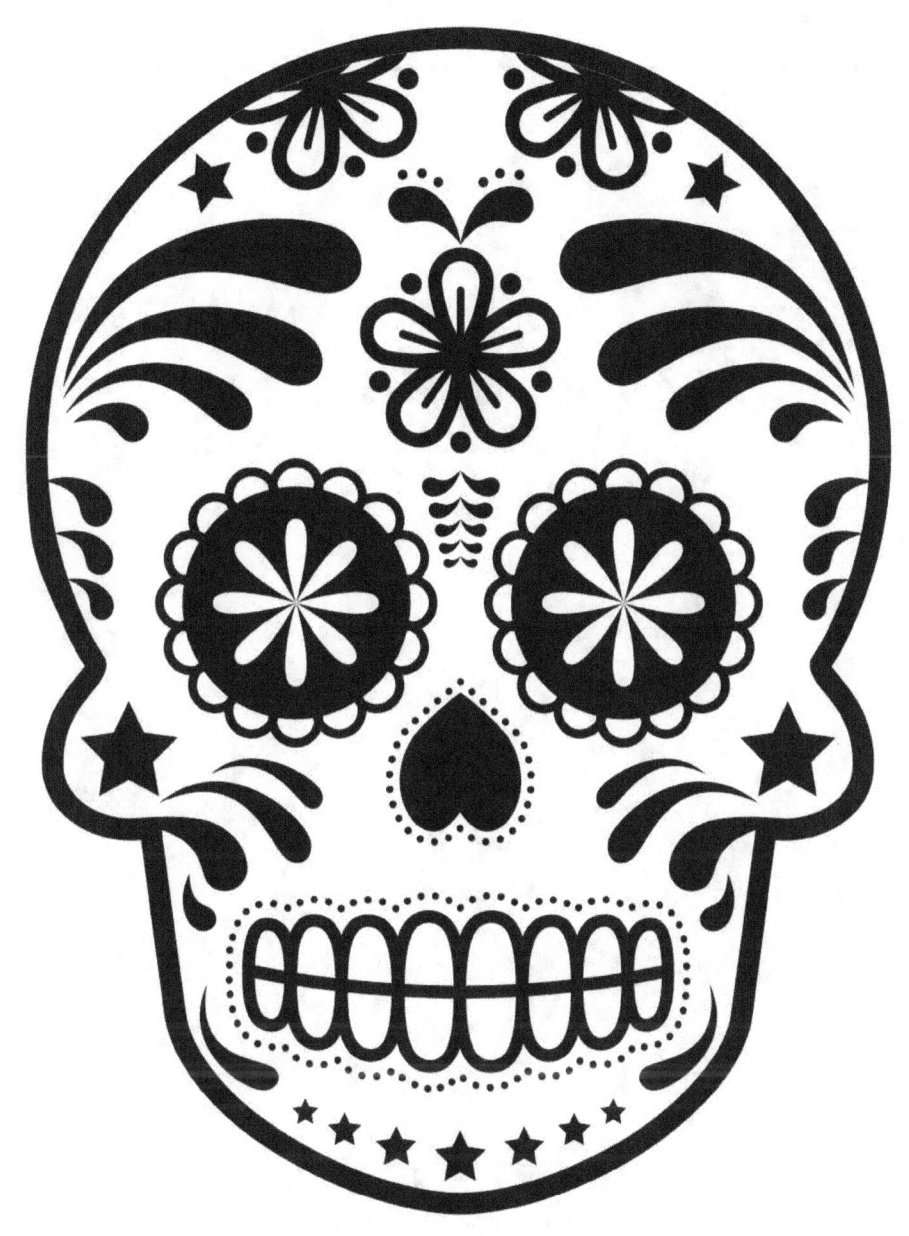

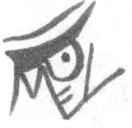

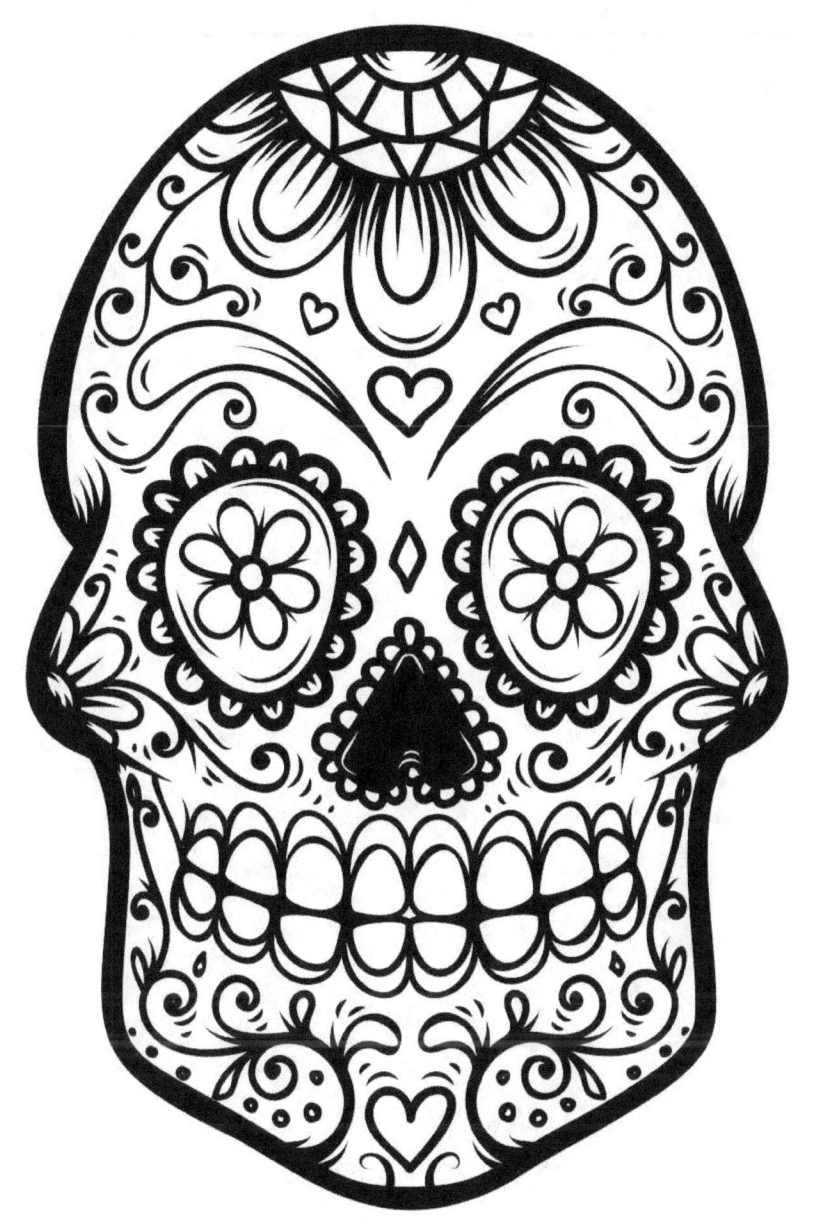
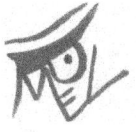

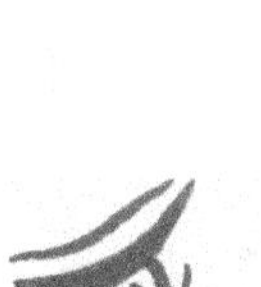

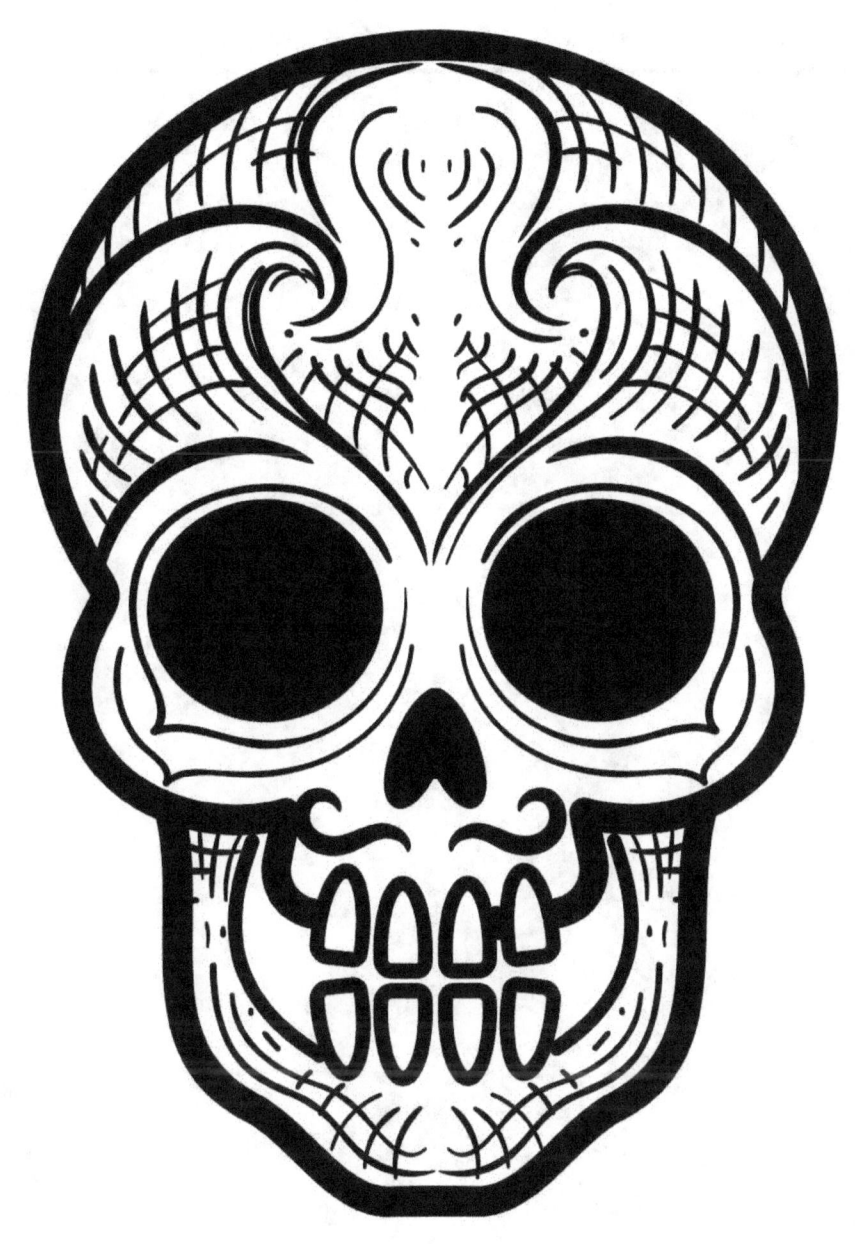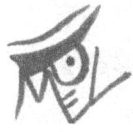

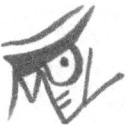

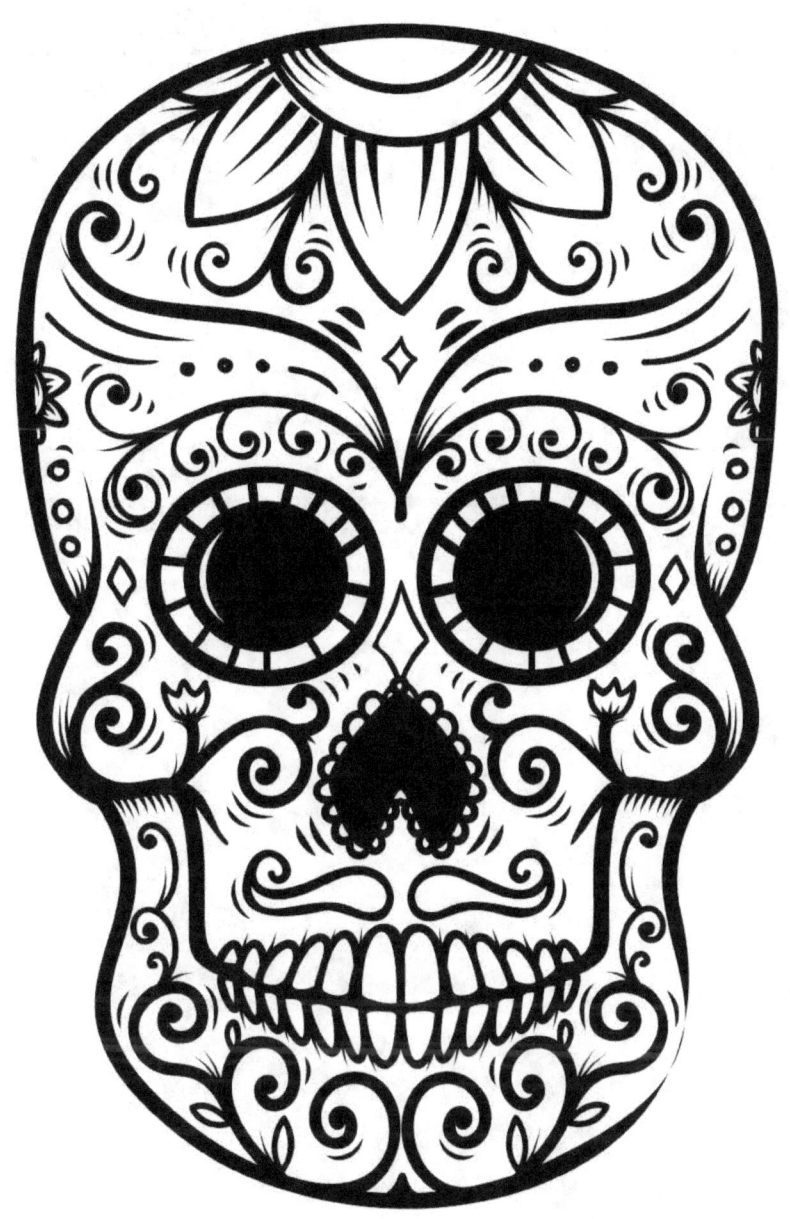

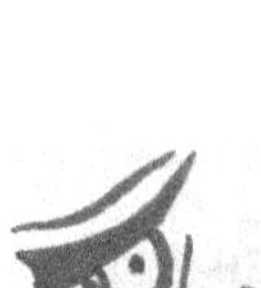

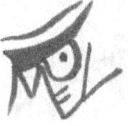

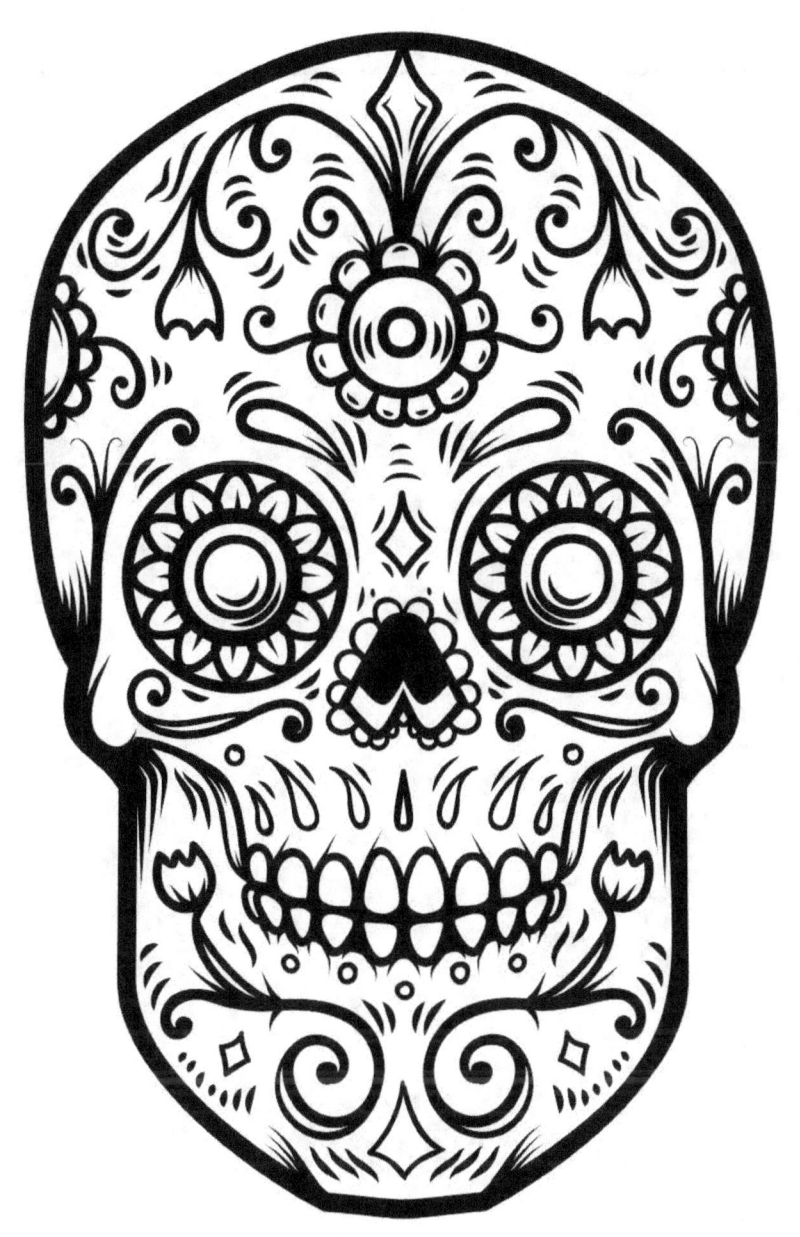

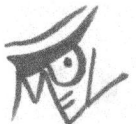

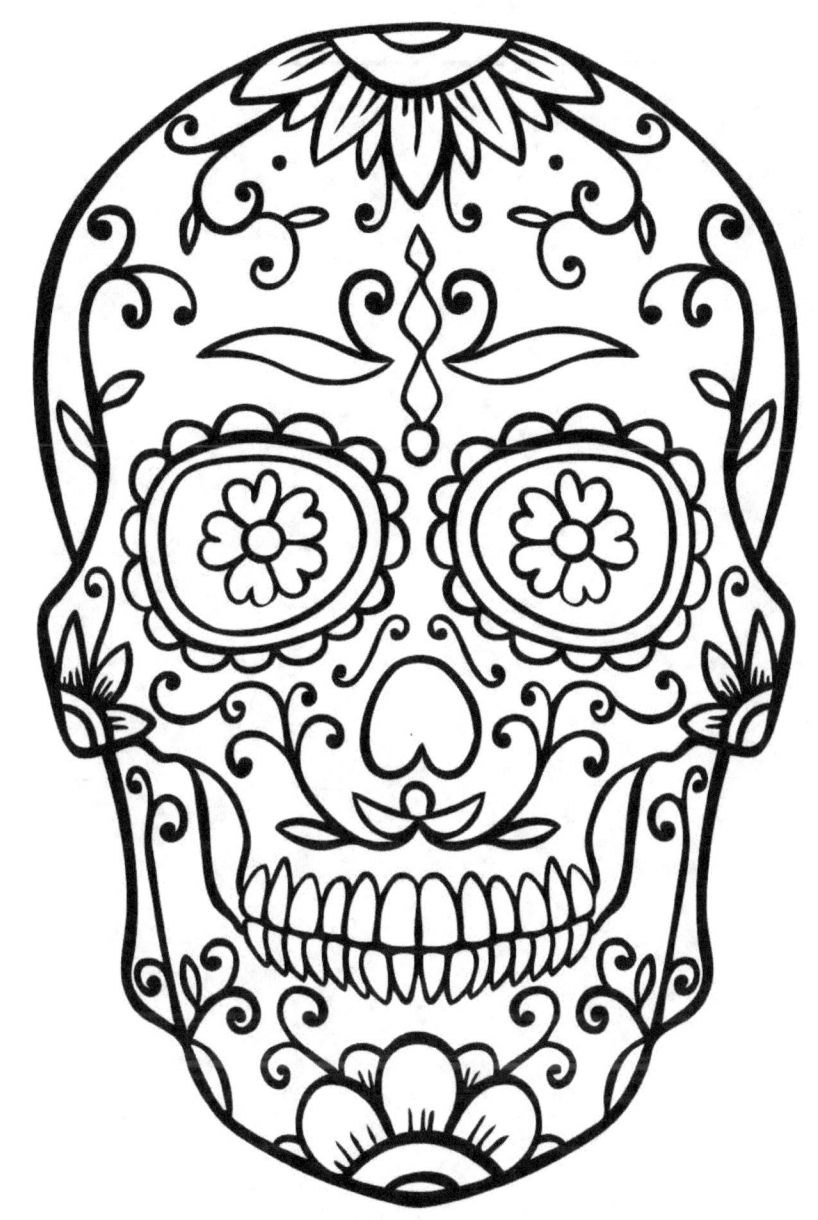

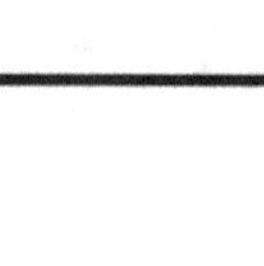

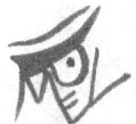

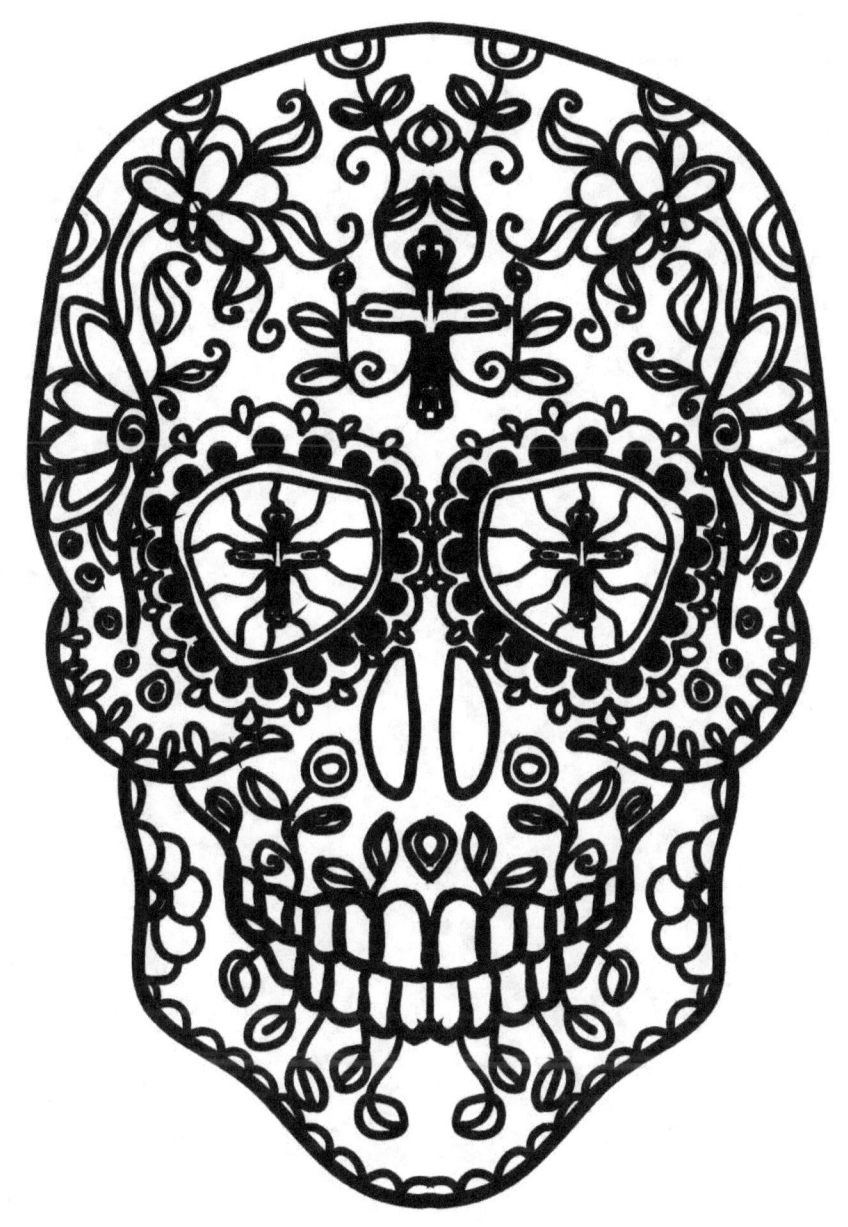
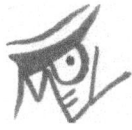

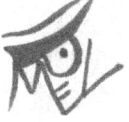

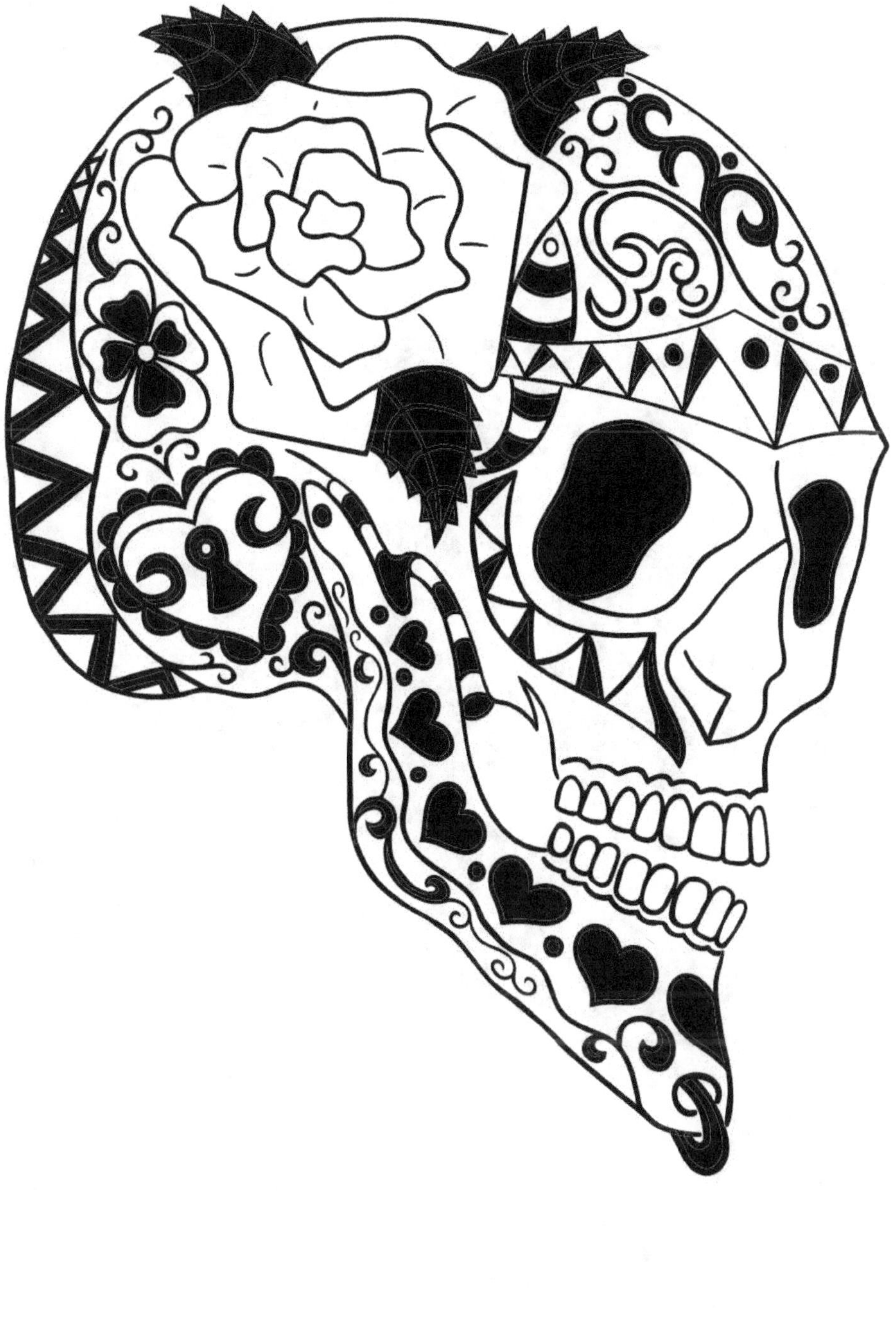

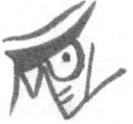

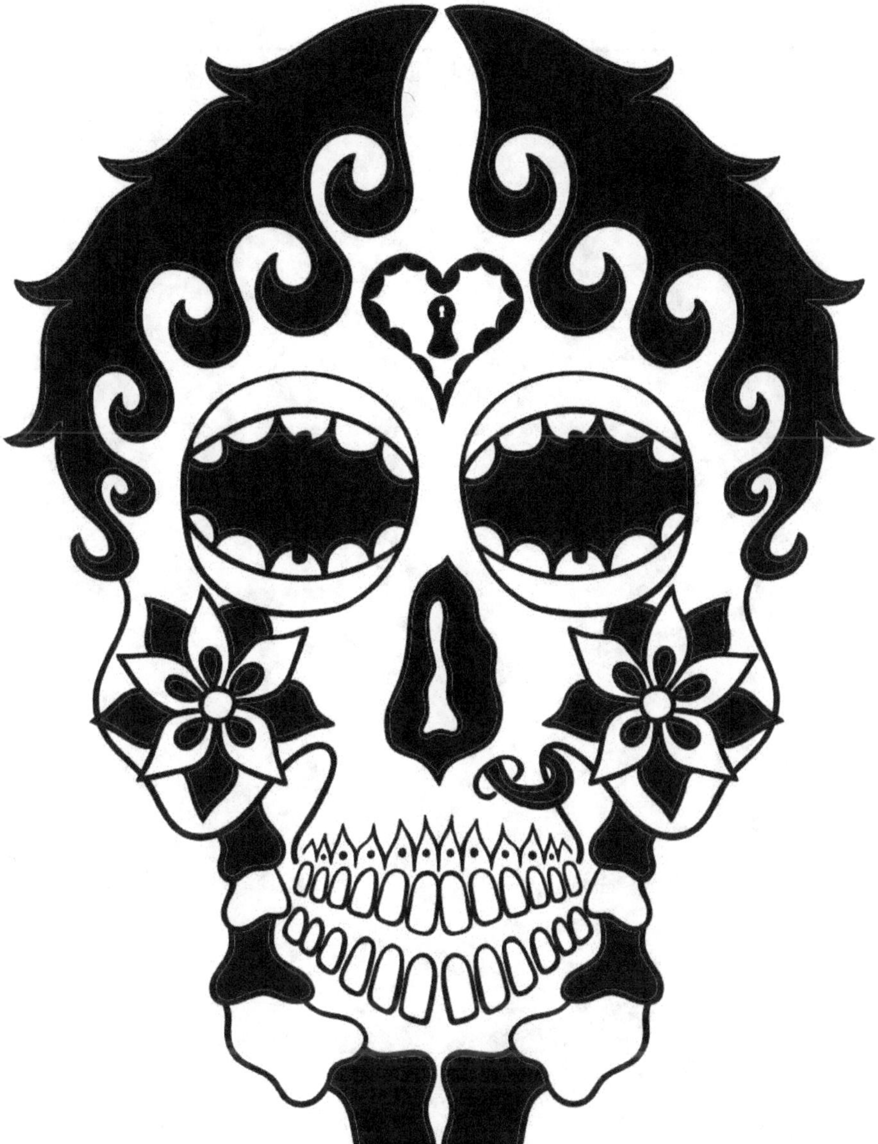

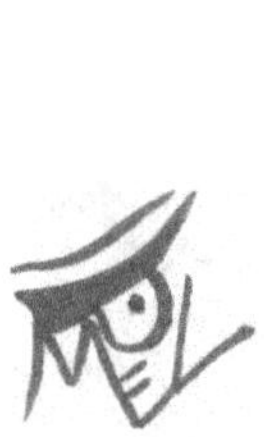

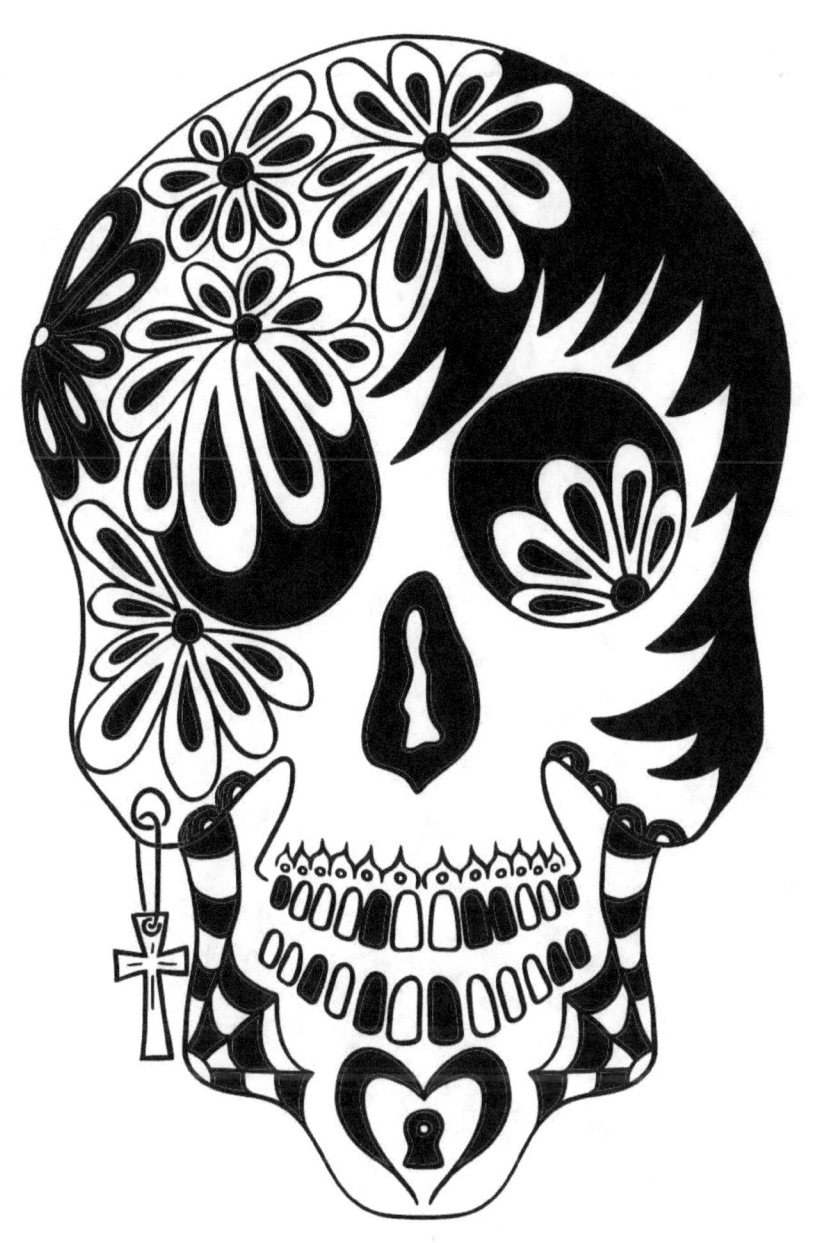

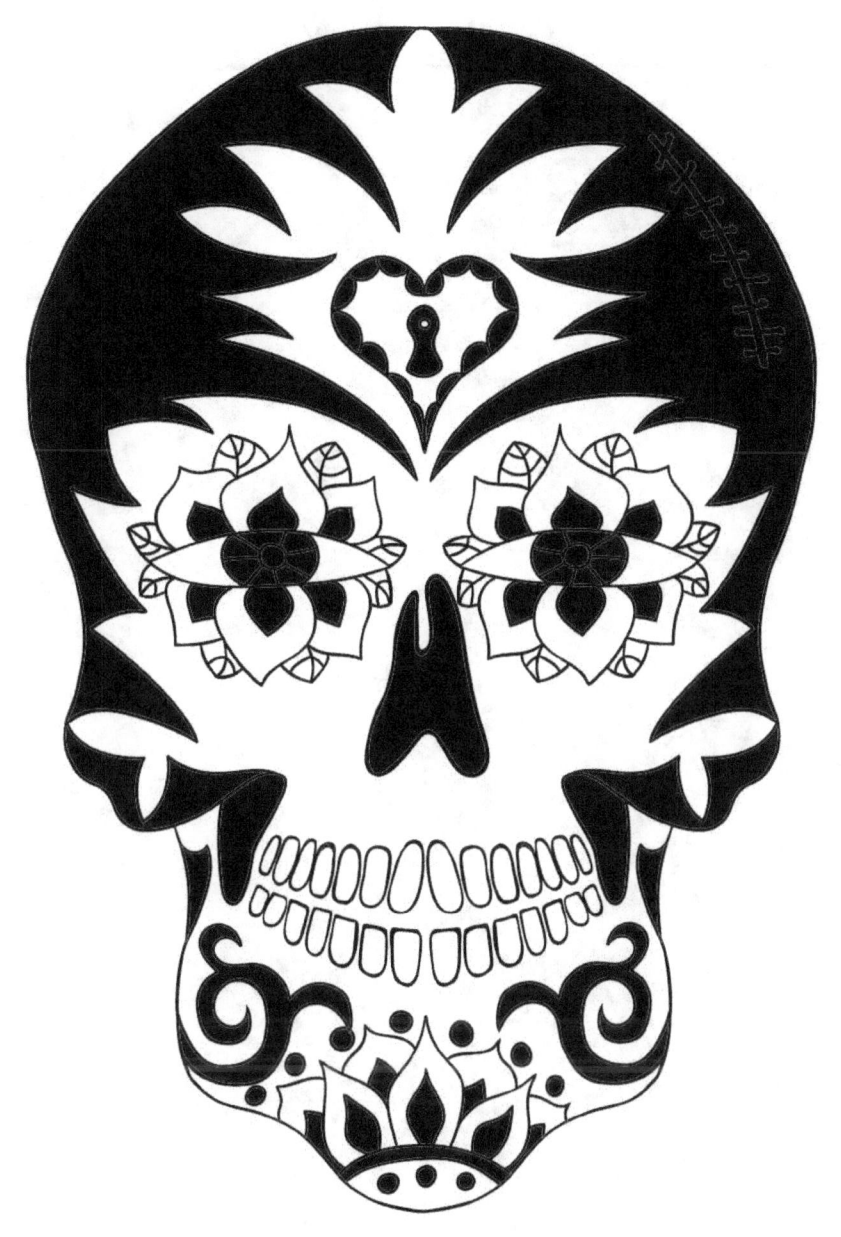

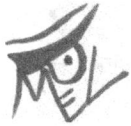

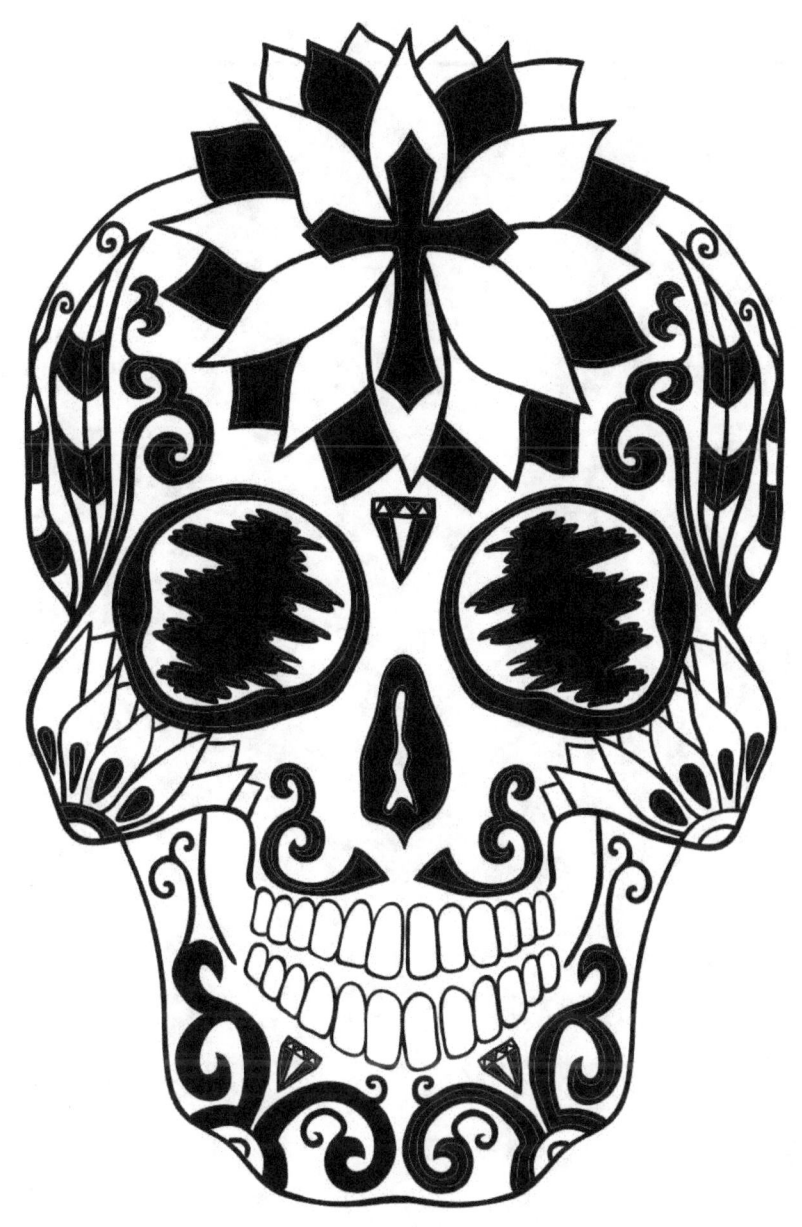

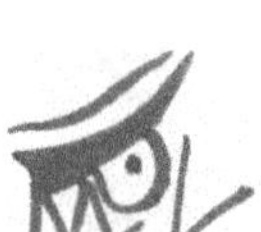

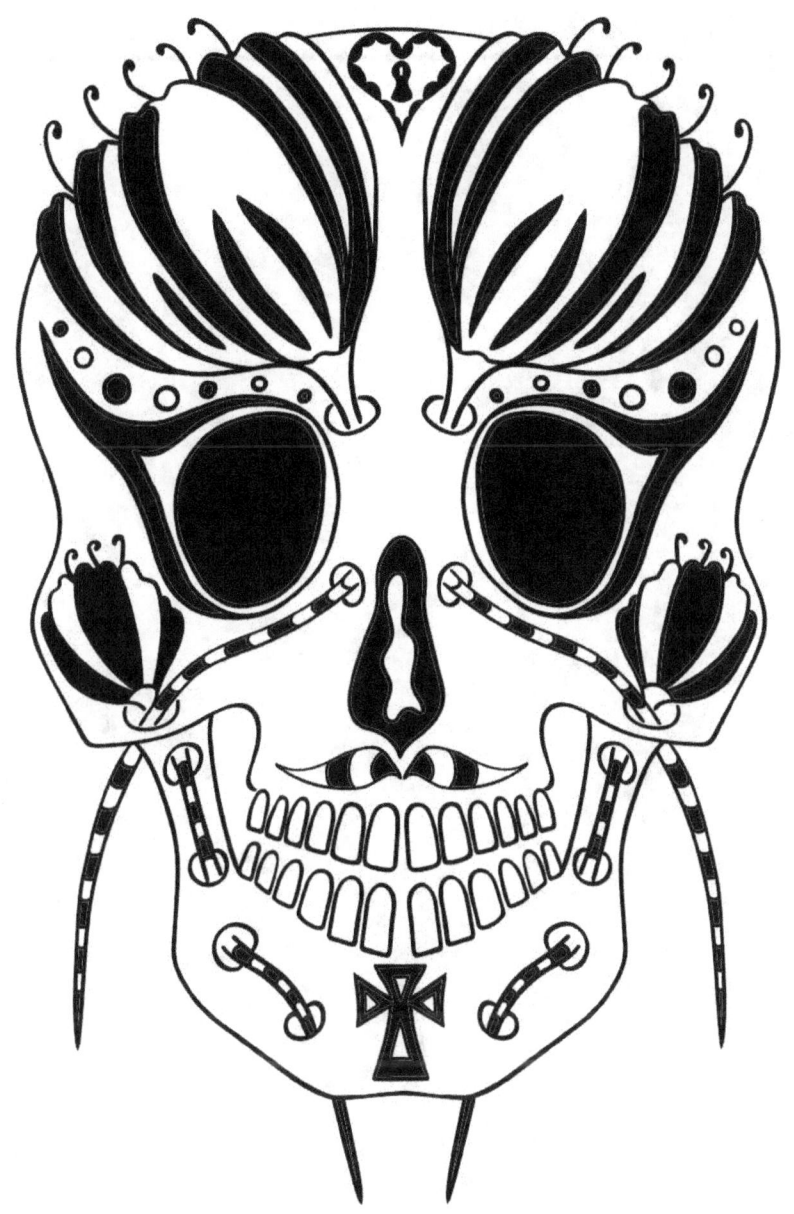

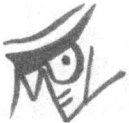

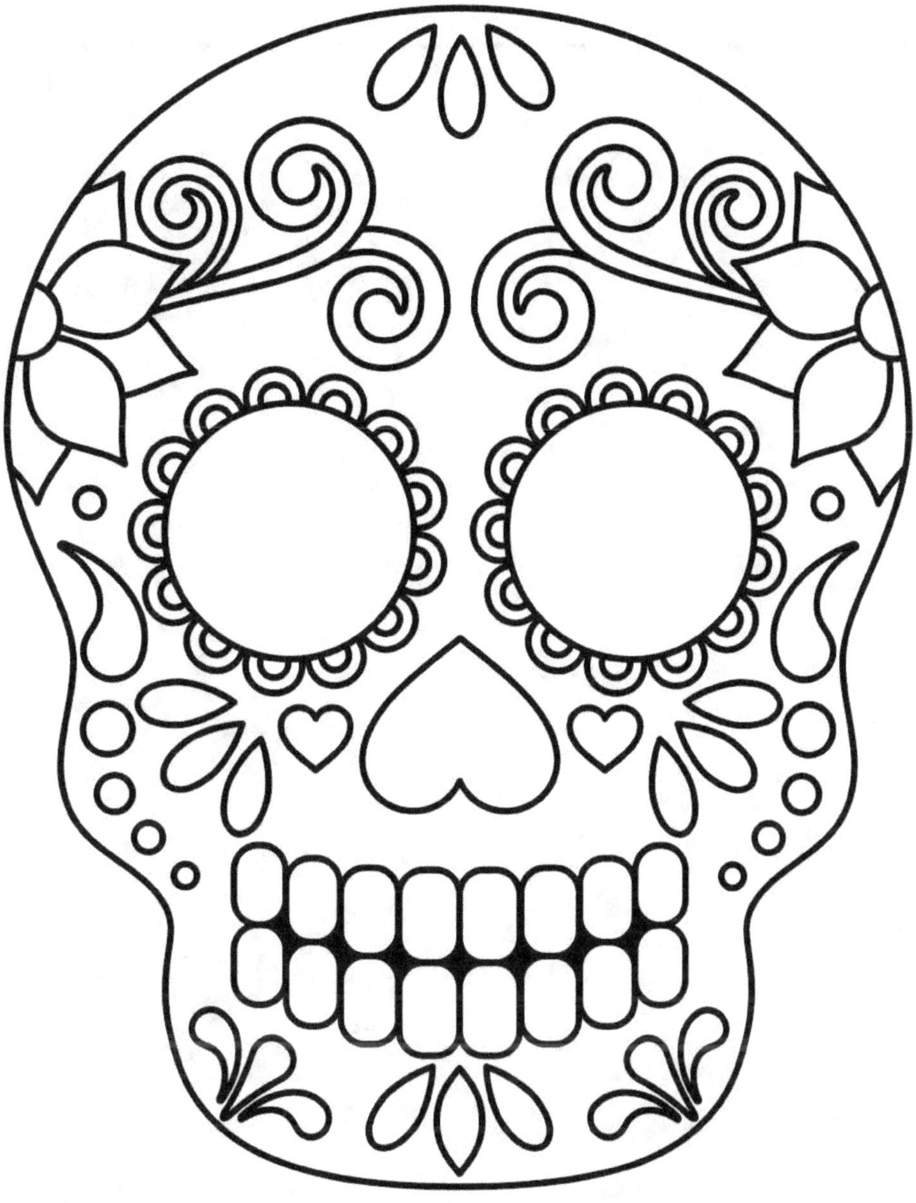

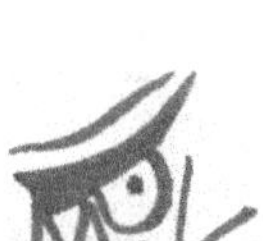

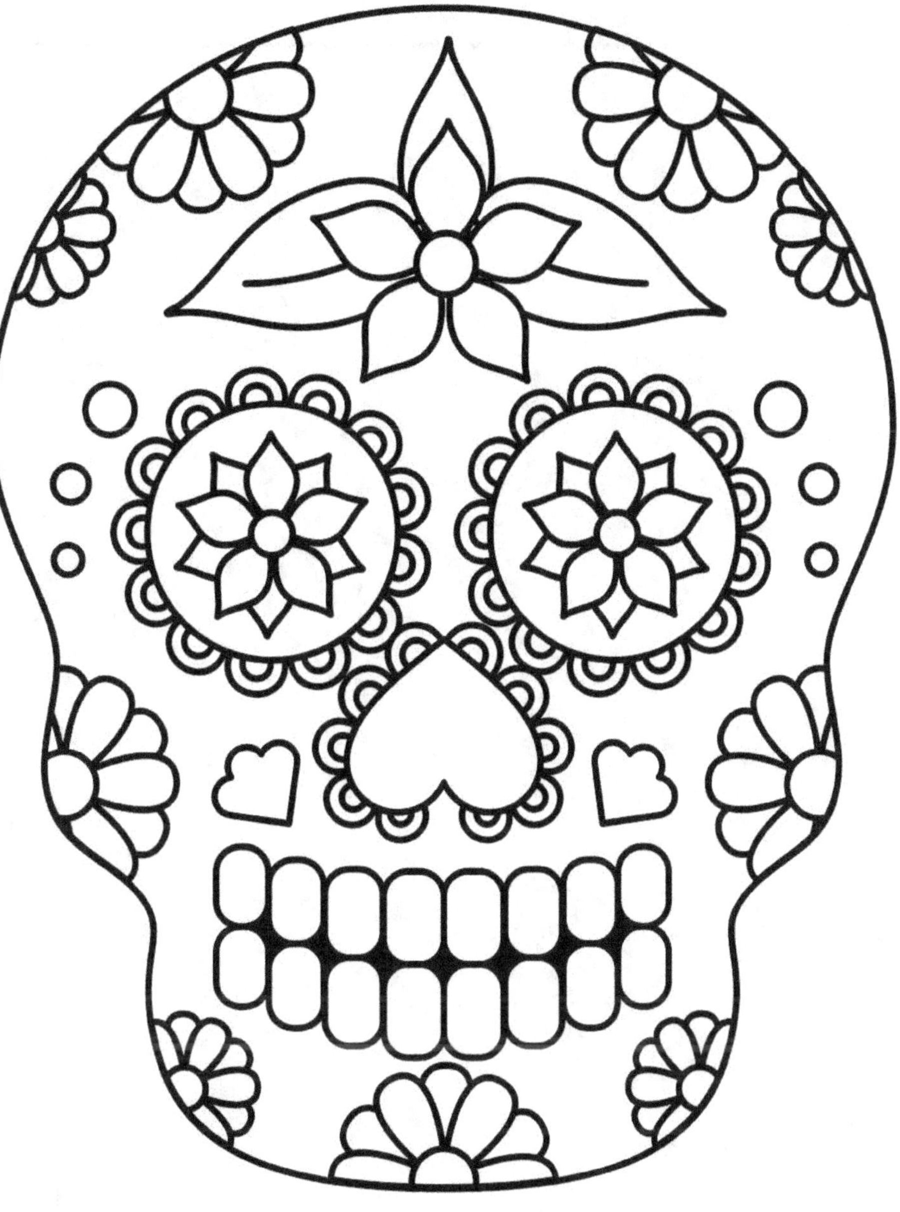

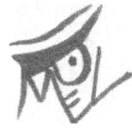

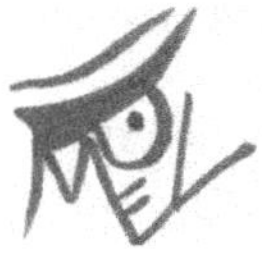

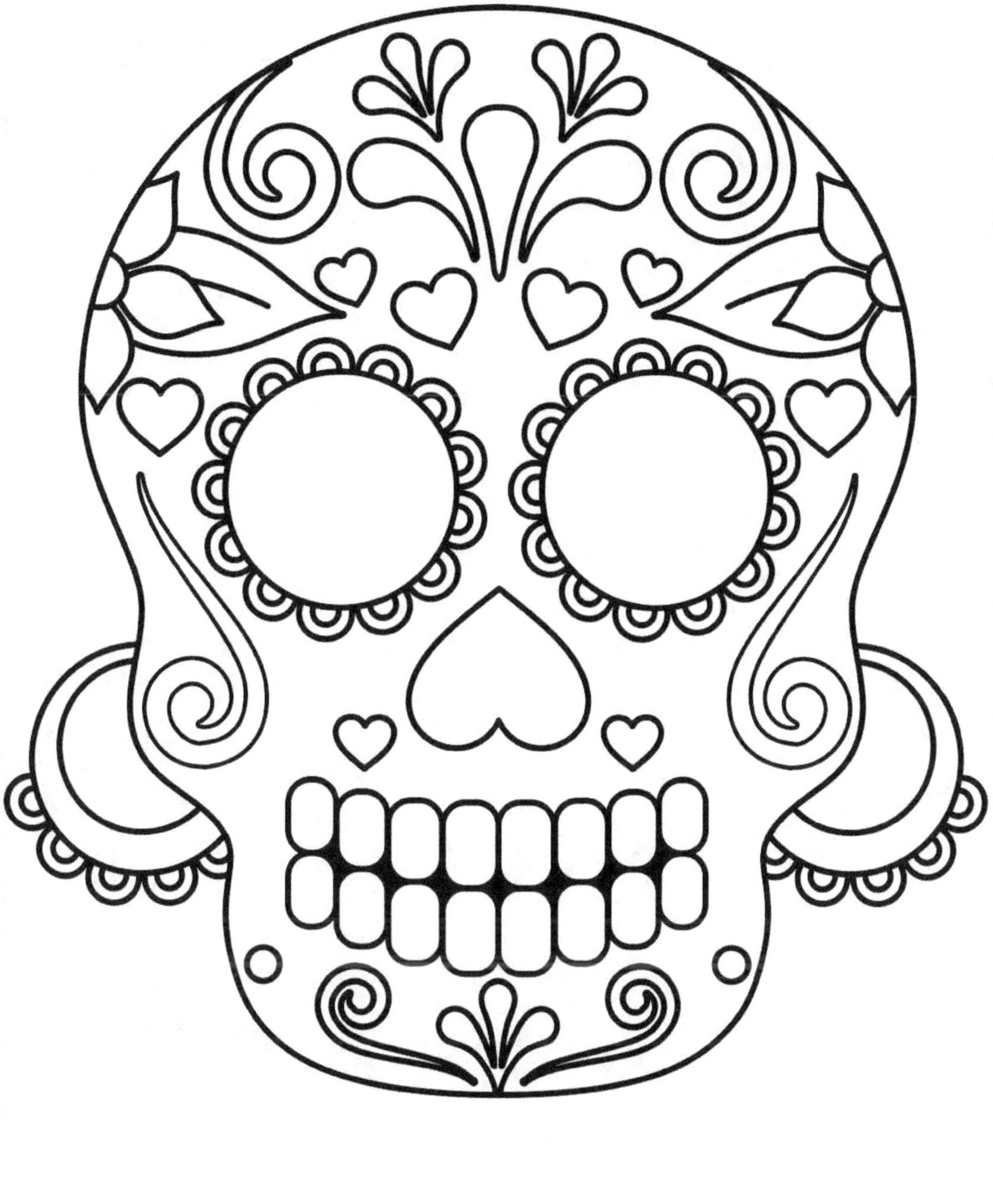

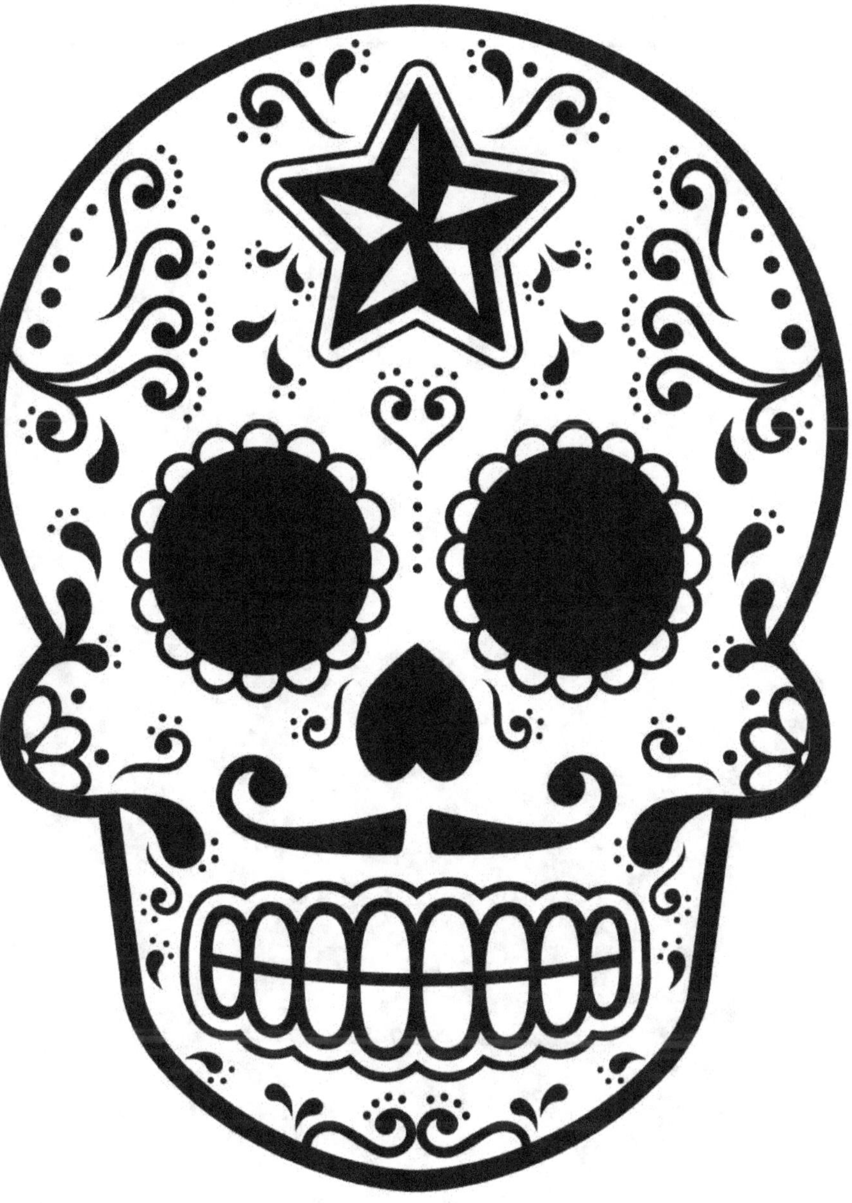

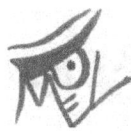

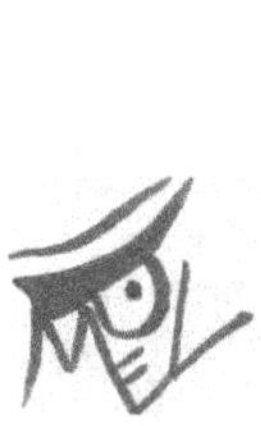

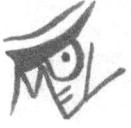

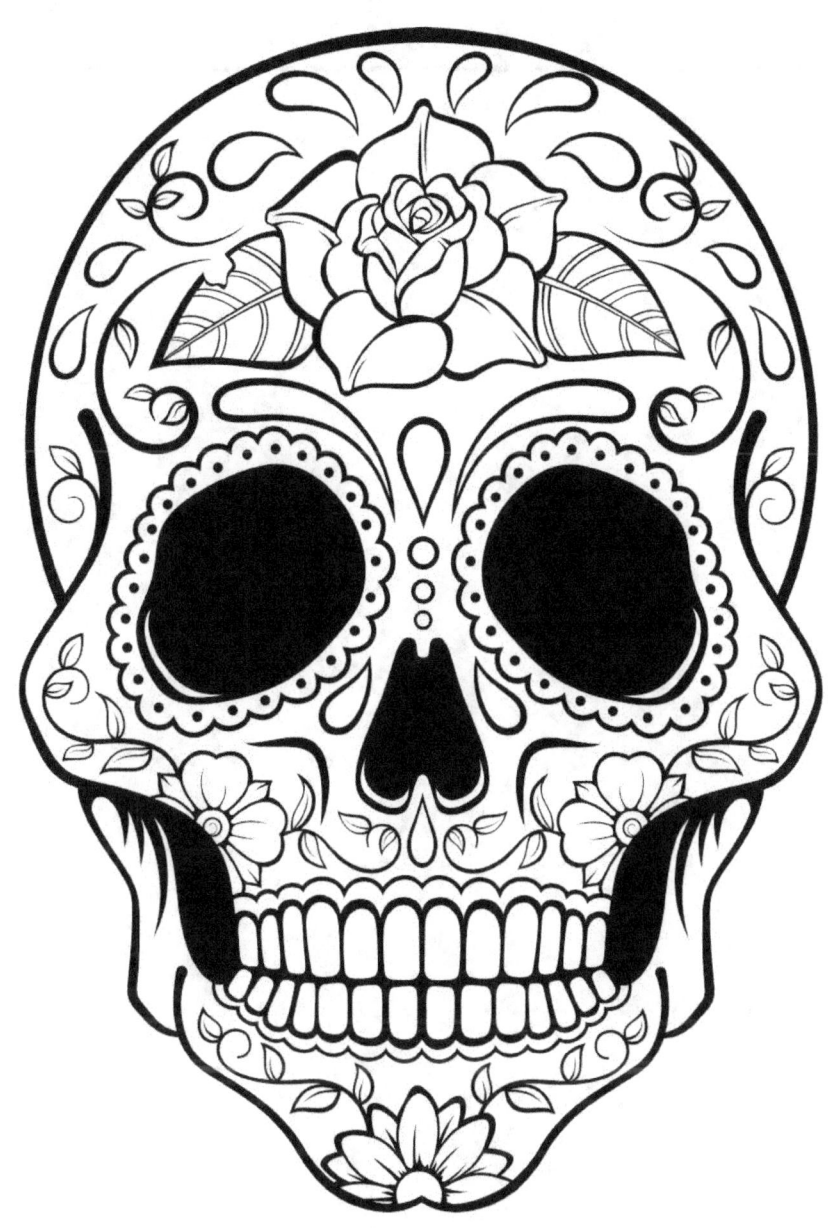

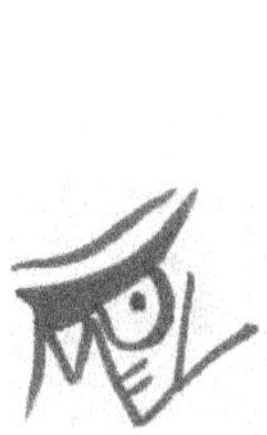

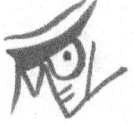

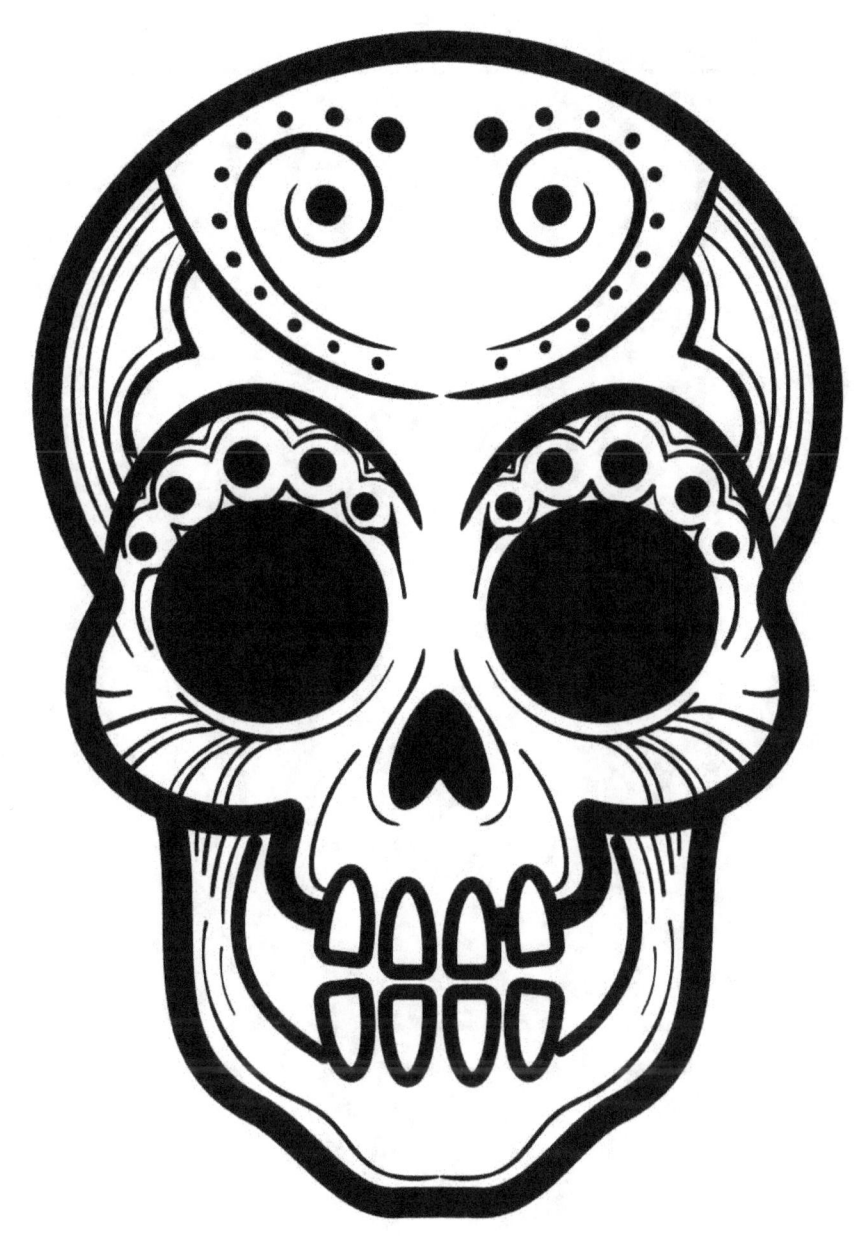

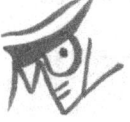

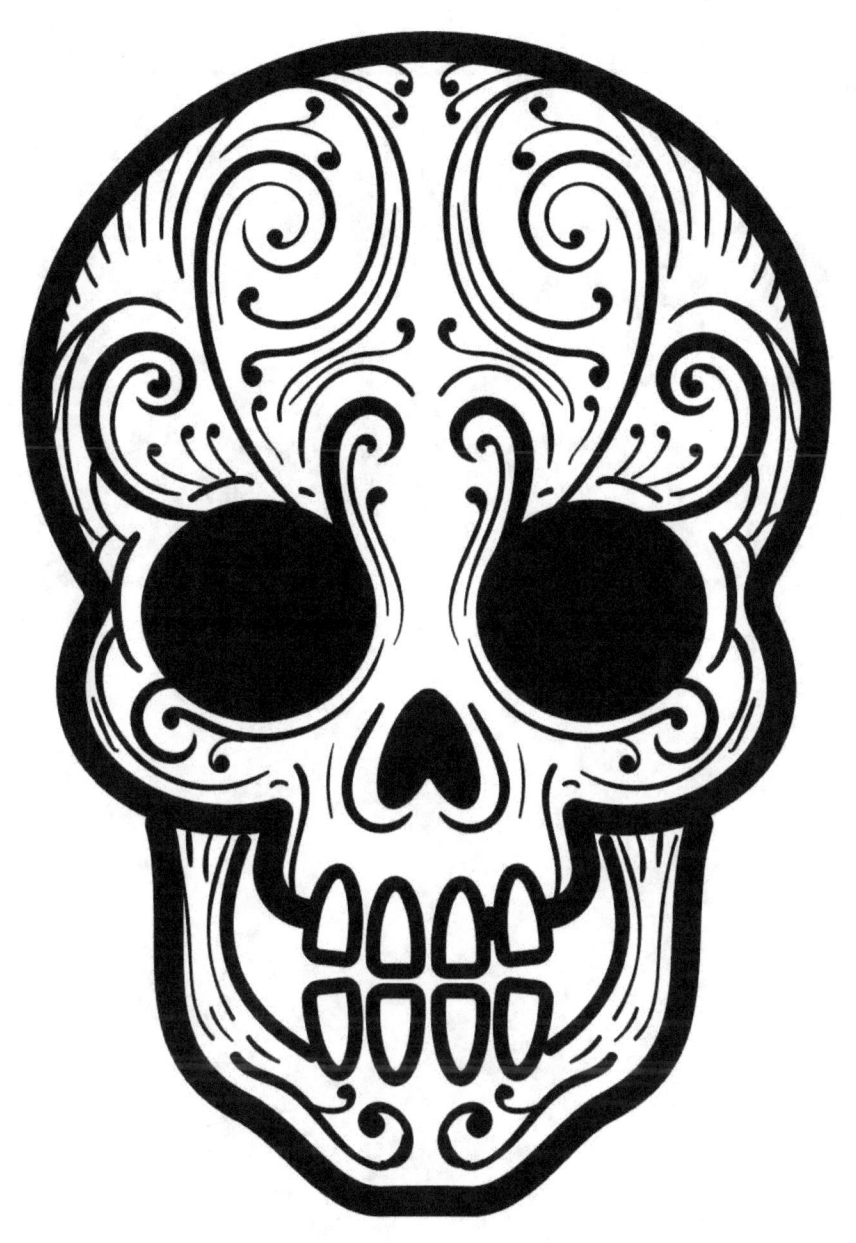
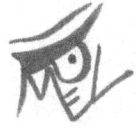

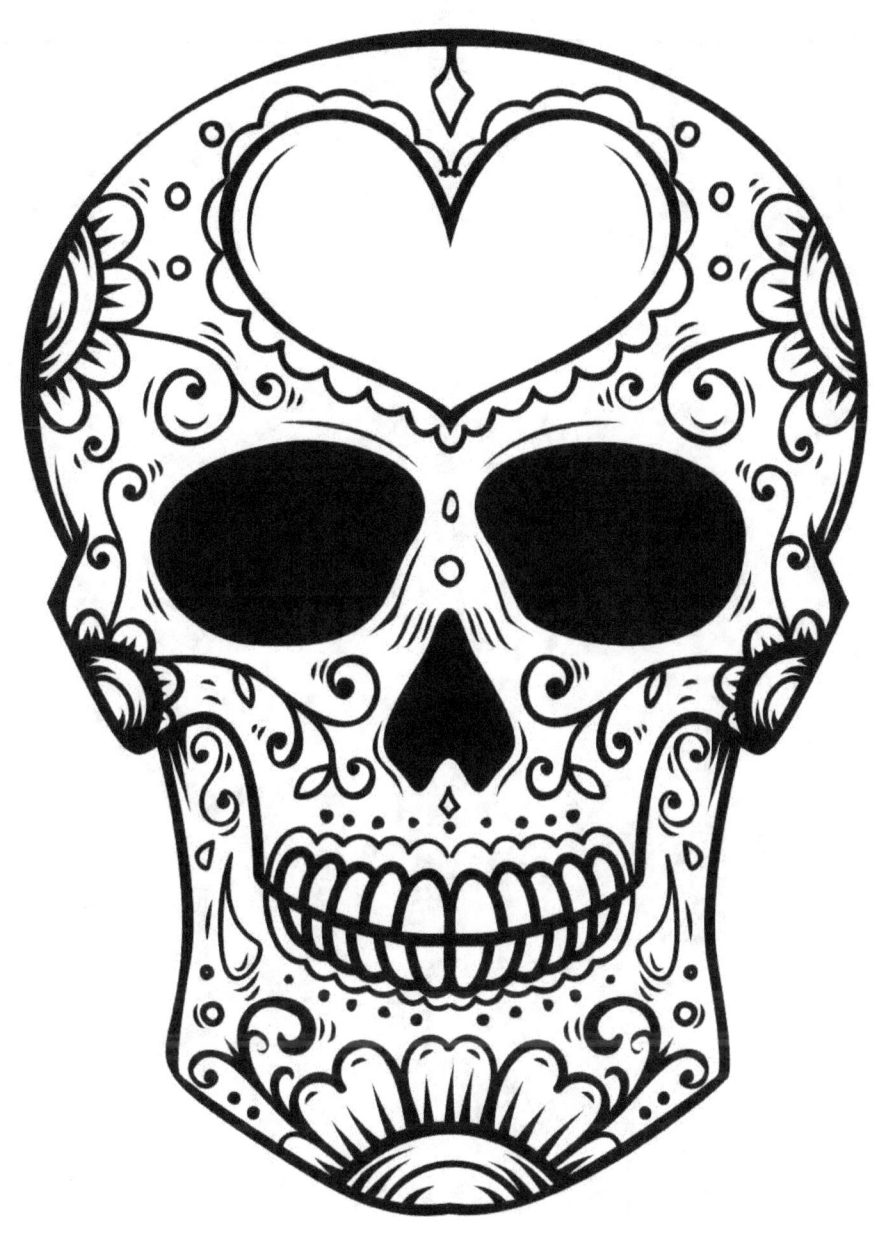
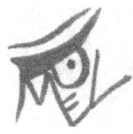

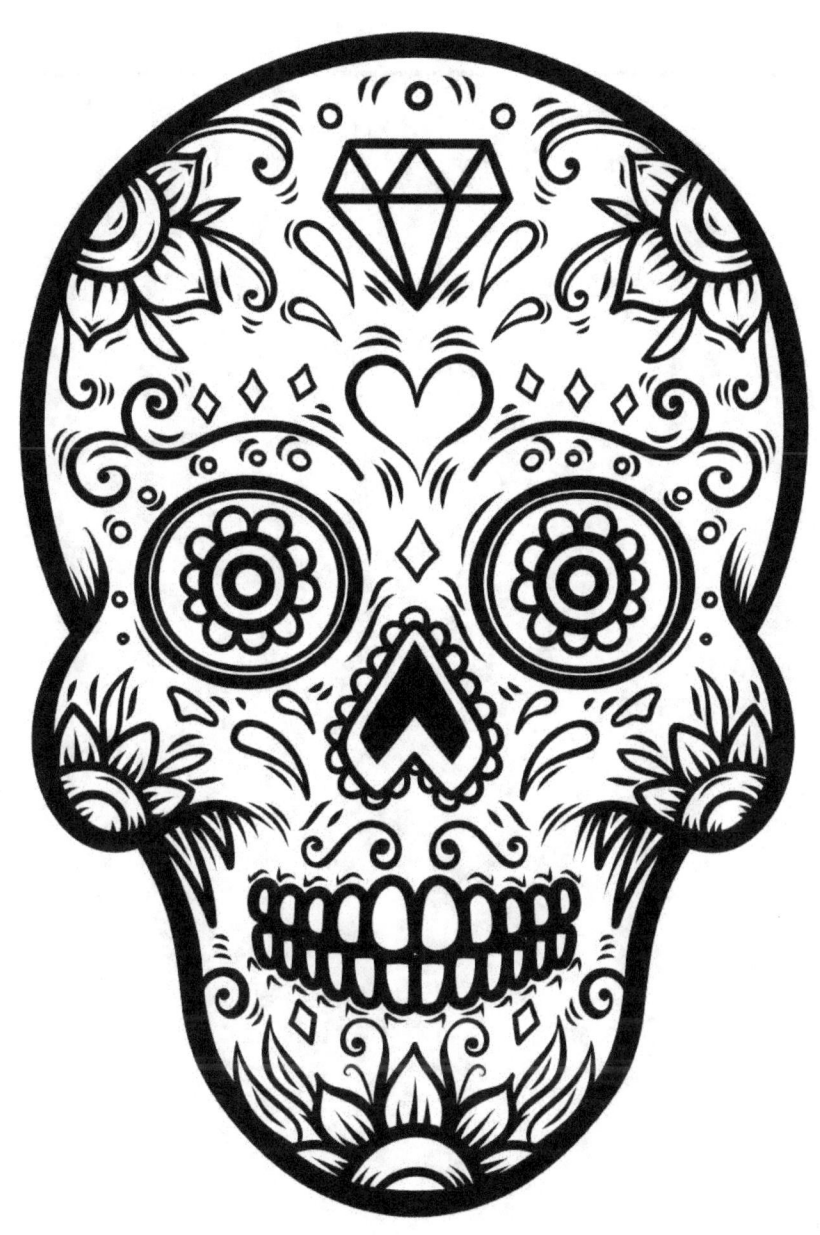

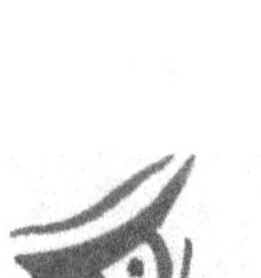

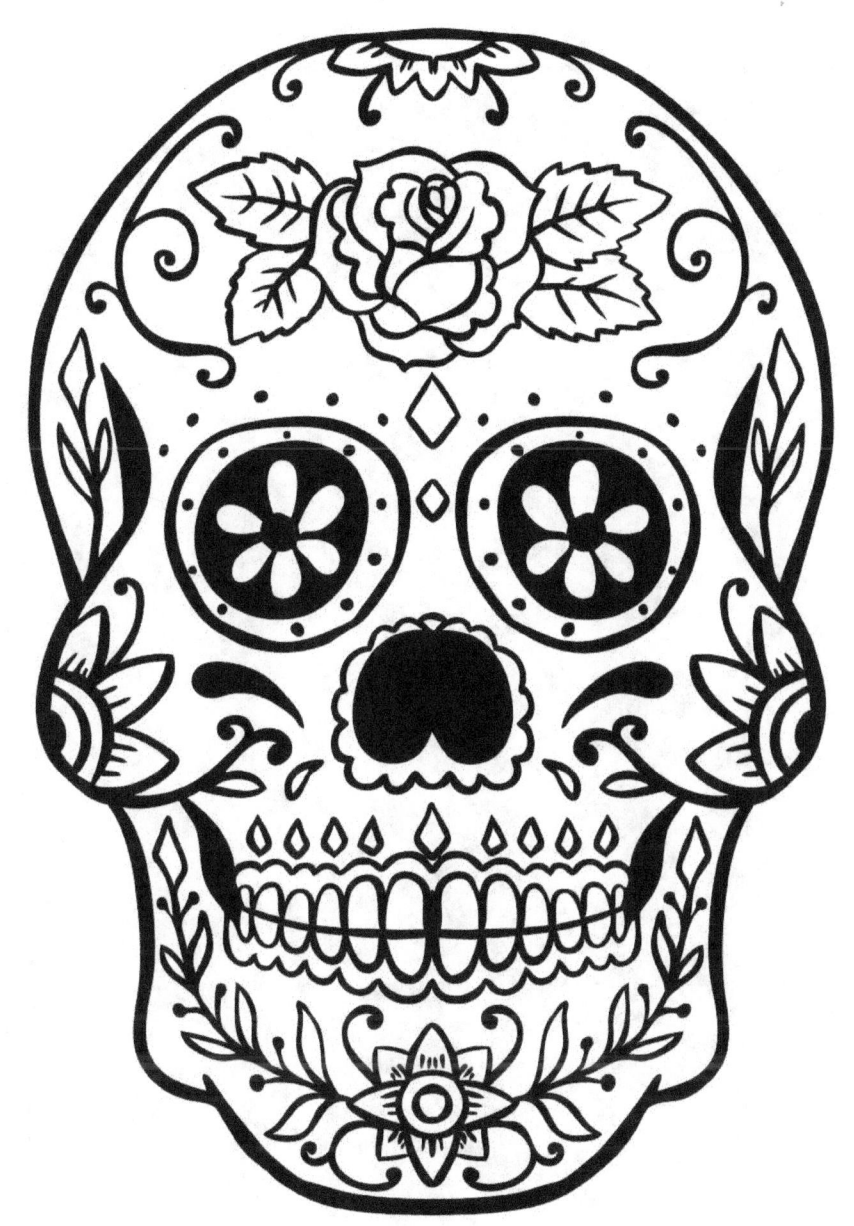

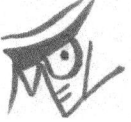

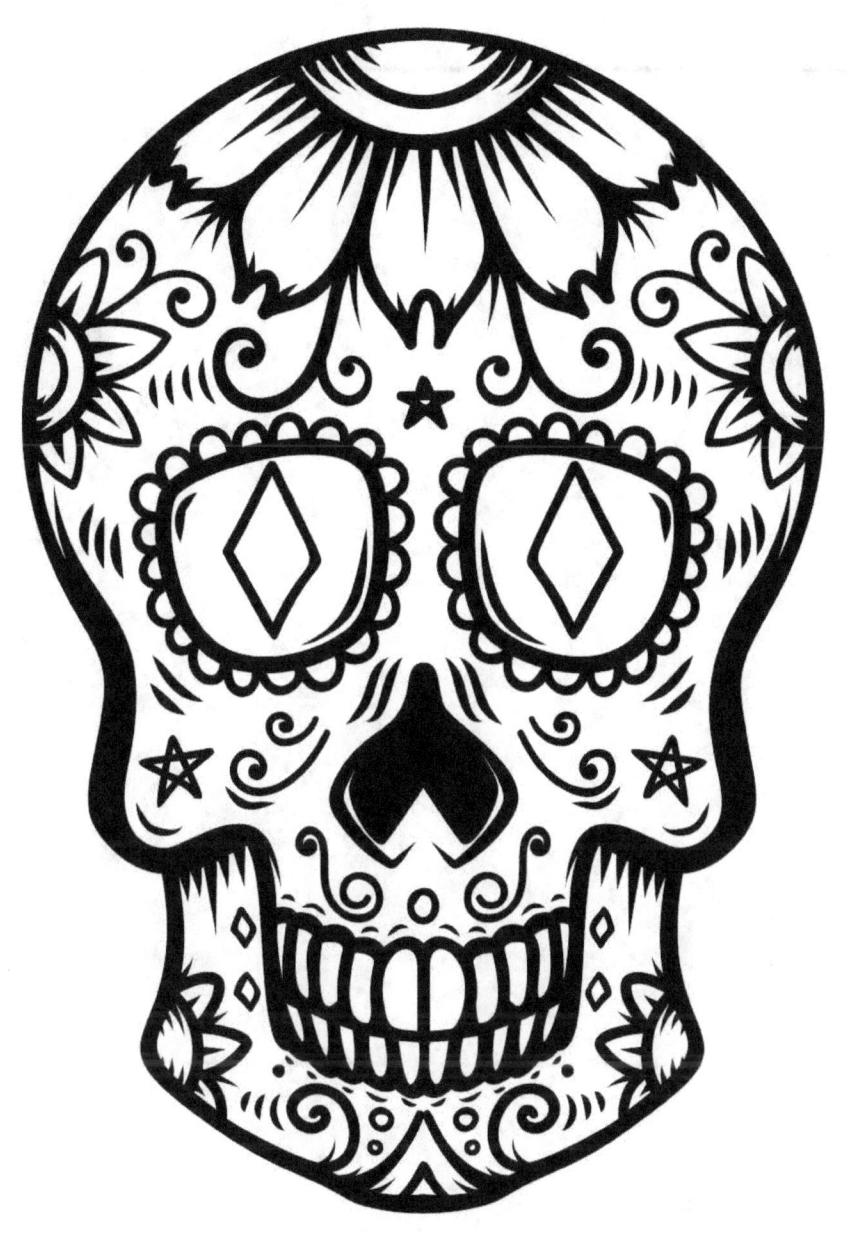

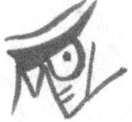

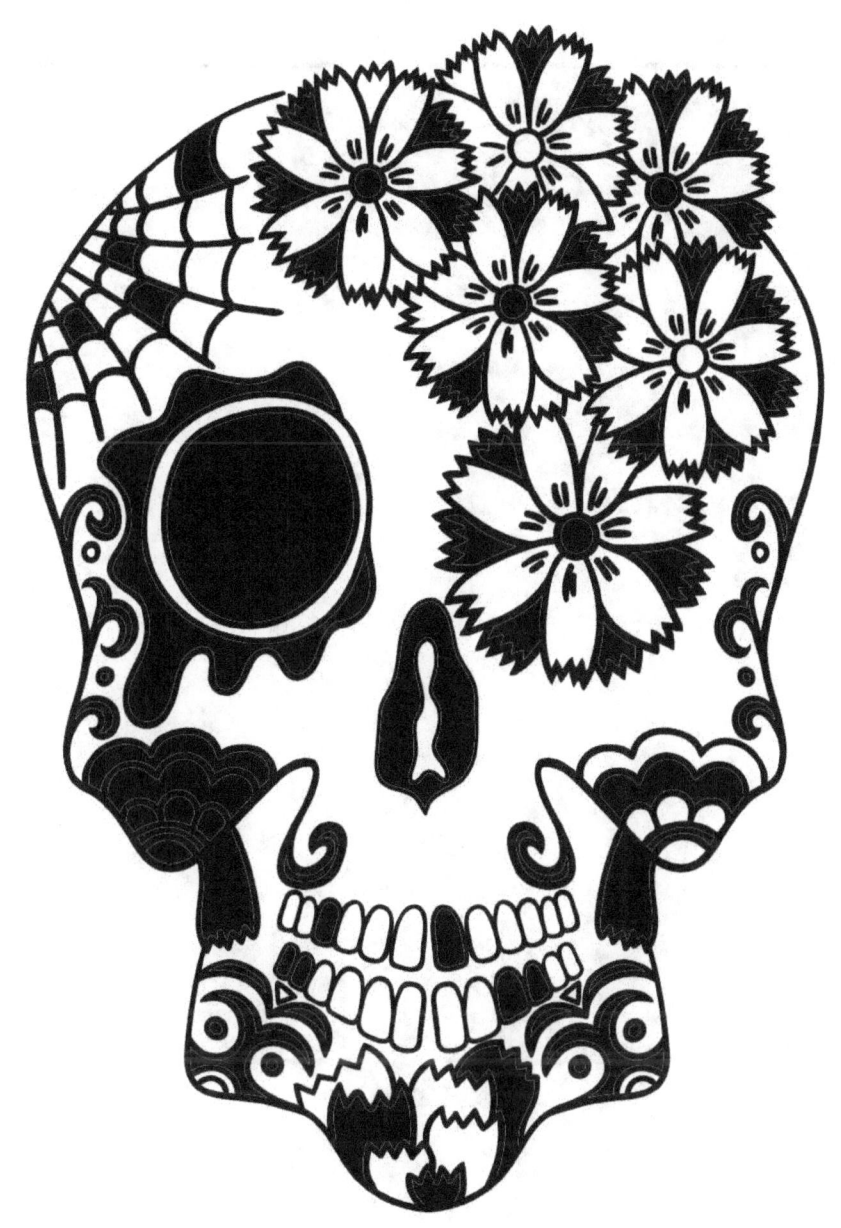
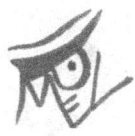

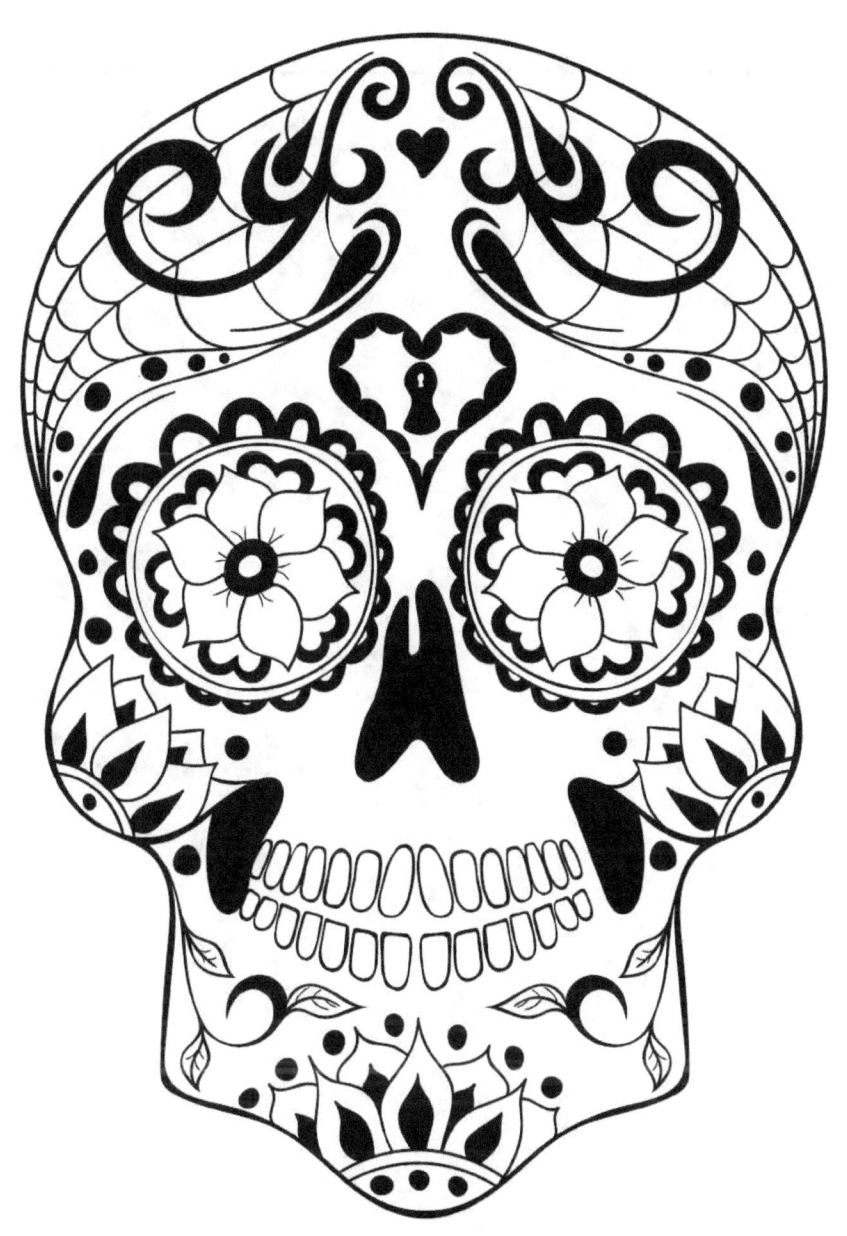

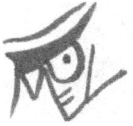

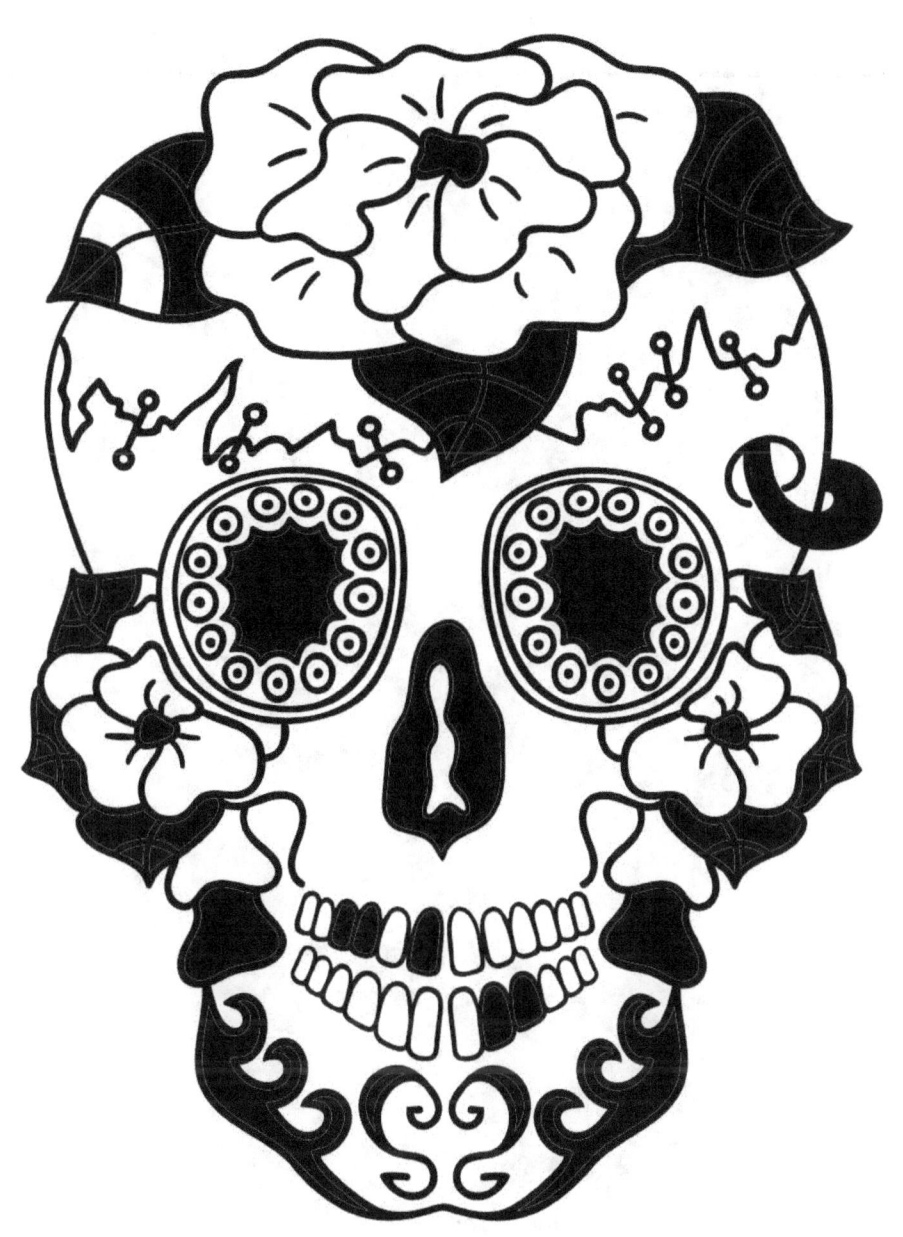

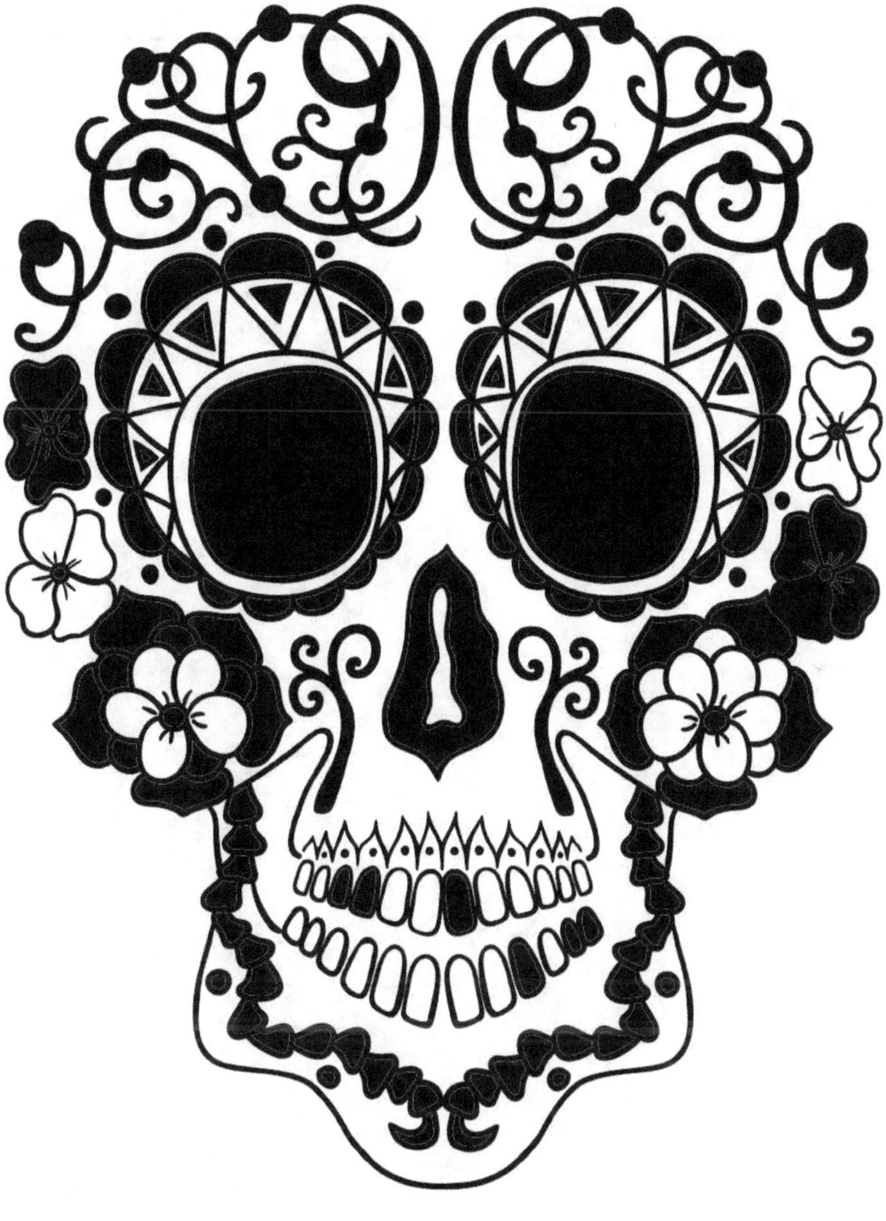

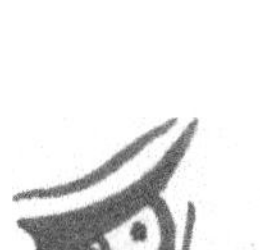

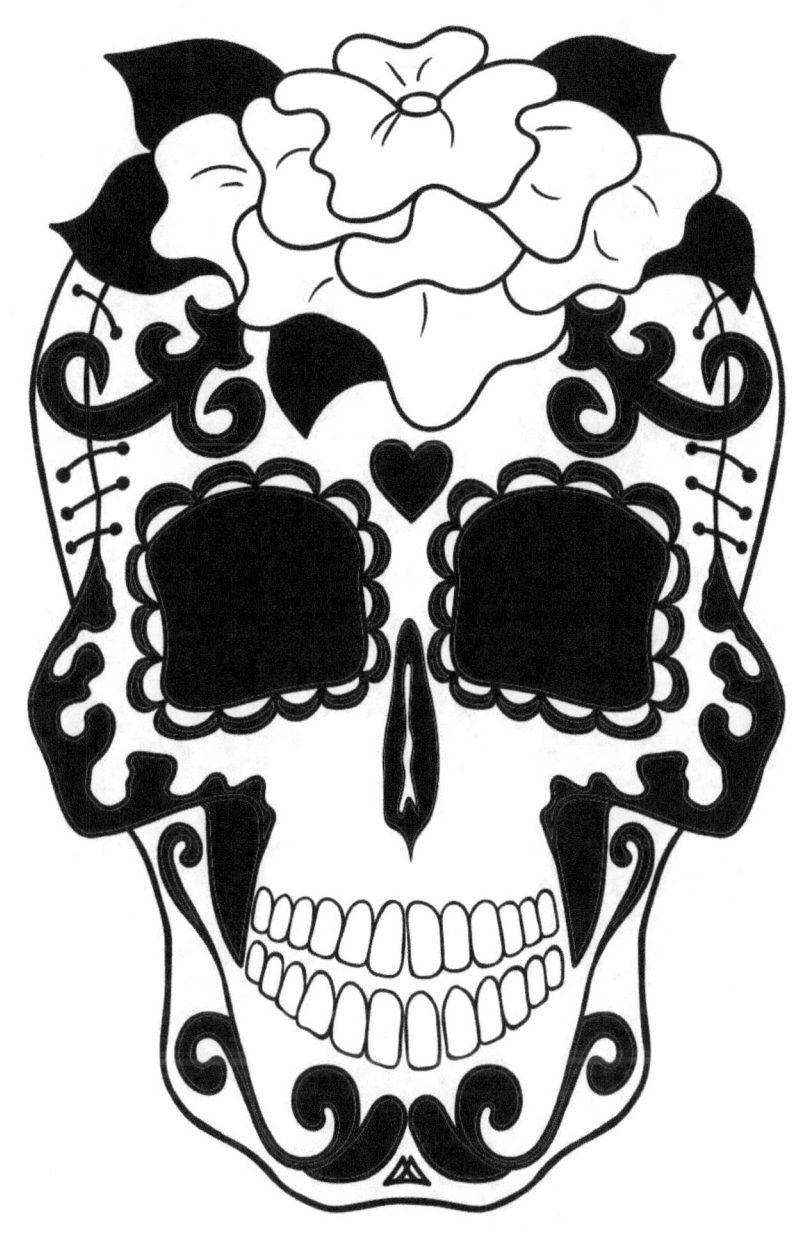

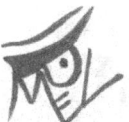

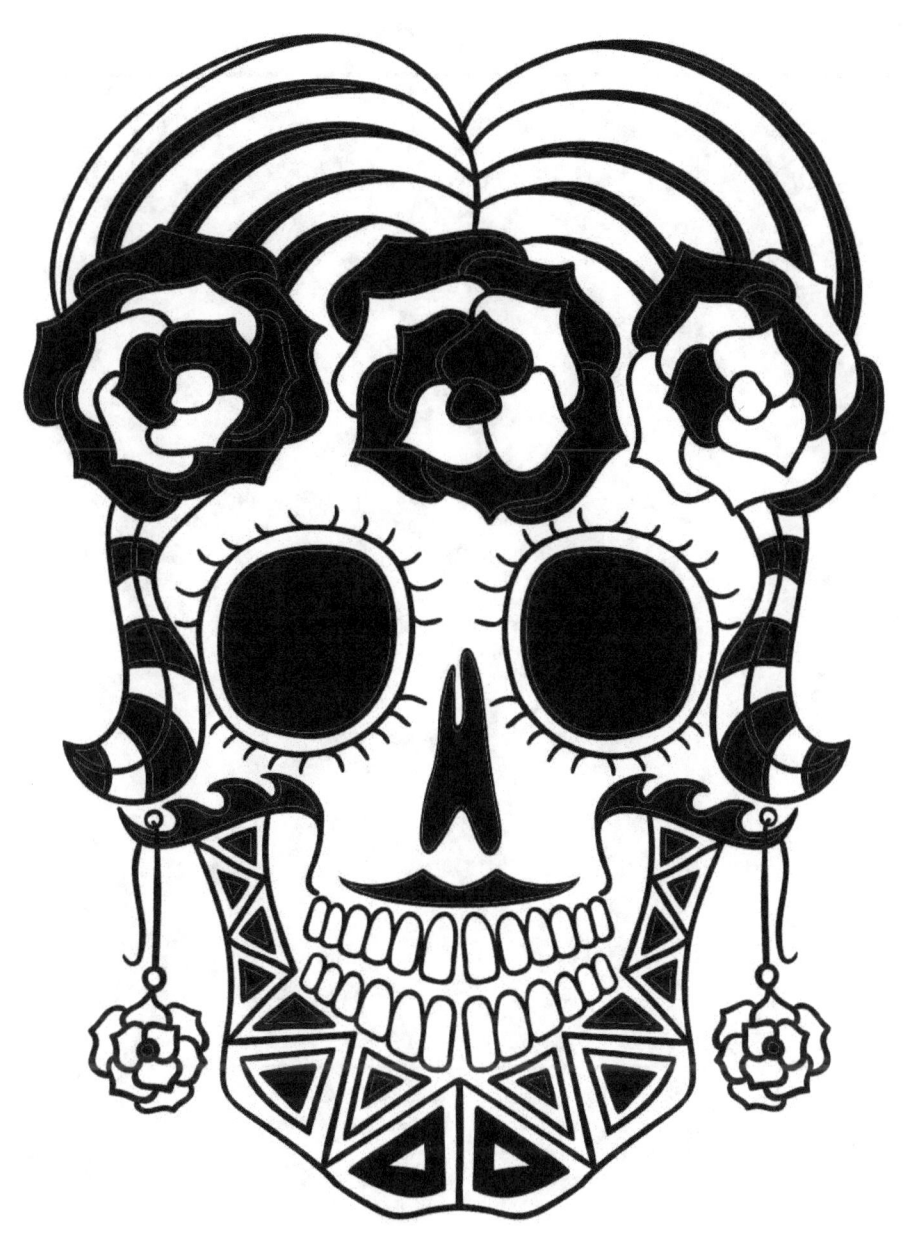

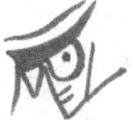

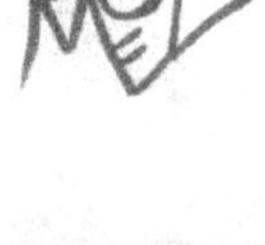

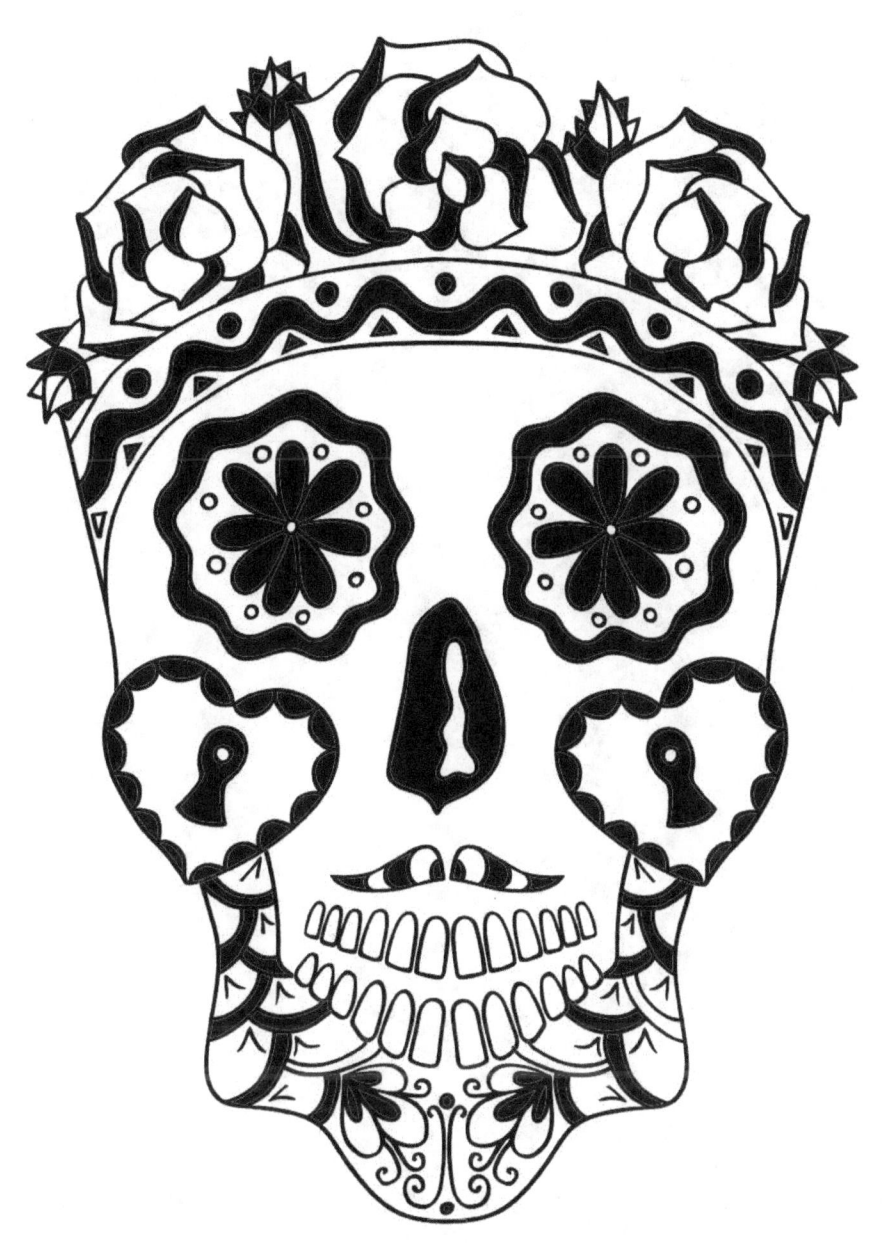

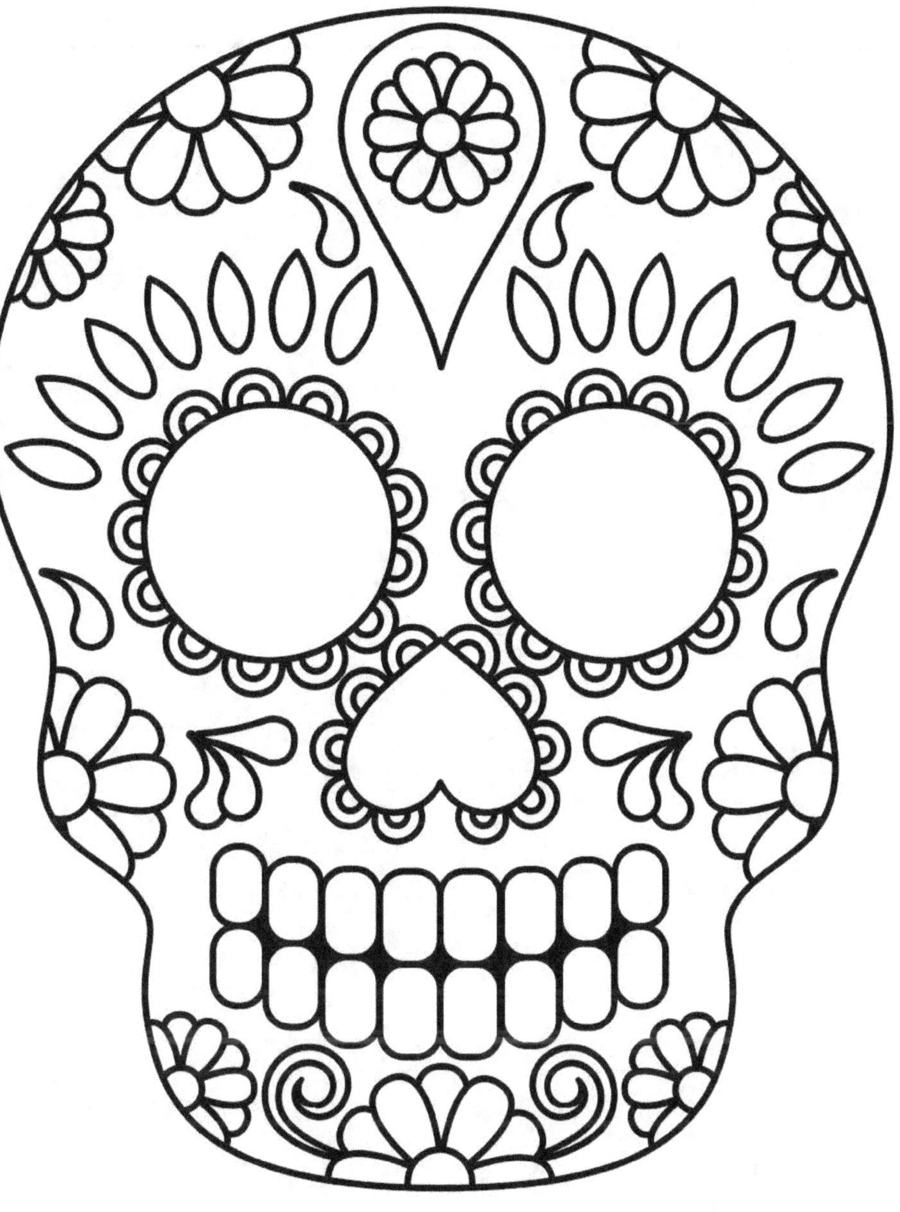

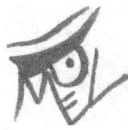

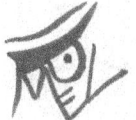

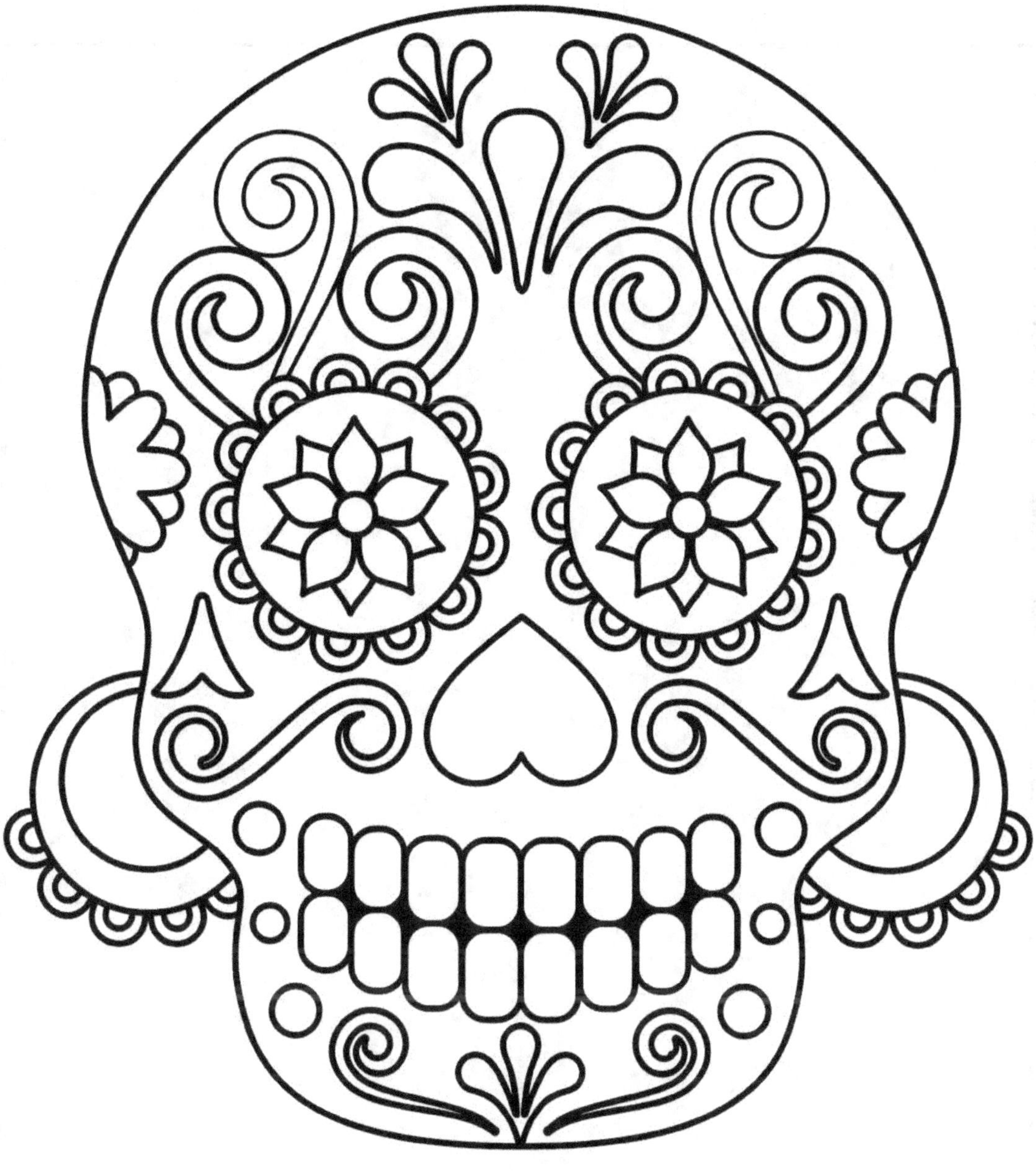

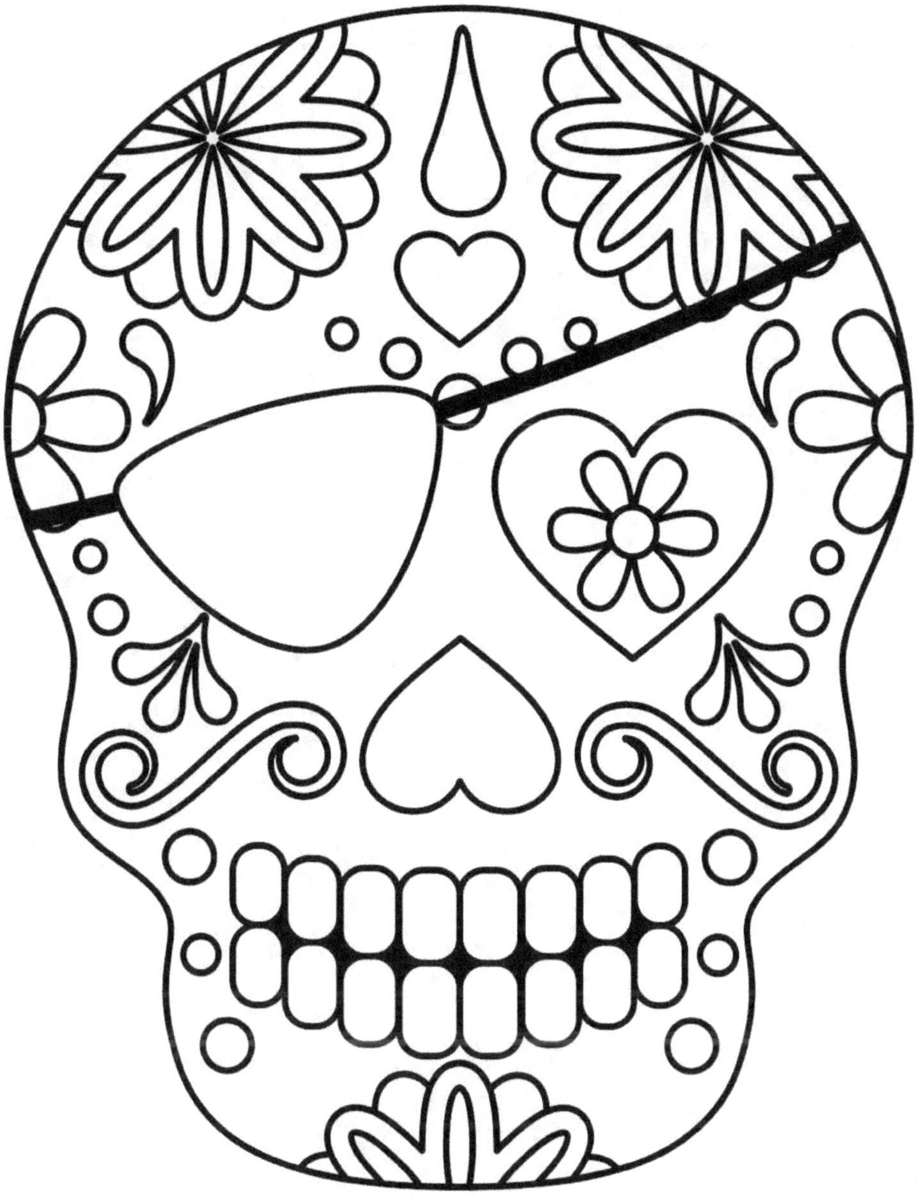

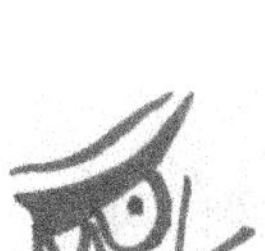

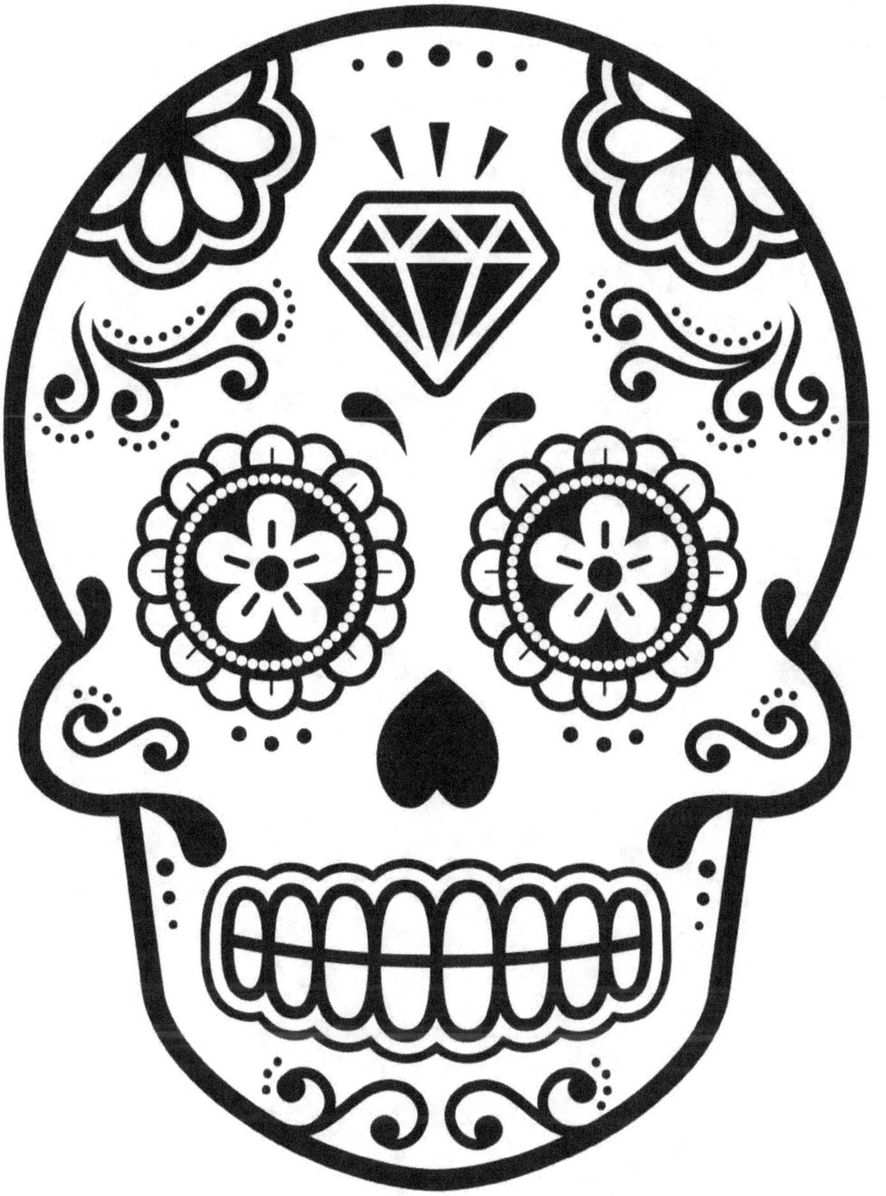

ADULT COLORING BOOKS BY MELISSA CAUDLE

Melissa Caudle has more adult coloring books available on Amazon, Barnes and Noble, and online retailers. You may also go to her website at:

www.drmelissacaudle.com

Abstract Faces Vols 1-5

Abstract Faces Carry Along Vol 1

Alien Faces Vols 1-2

Hippie Power

Cubism Faces

Pretty Faces

Sugar Skull Coloring Book

ORIGINAL ART BY MELISSA CAUDLE

Melissa Caudle sells her original art from her website: www.drmelissacaudle.com. Several of the original drawings included in this book, colored by the artist, may still be available for sale. They are a collector's item. All art is accompanied by a Certificate of Authenticity and signed by the artist.

CONTACT INFORMATION

Website: www.drmelissacaudle.com

Email: drmelcaudle@icloud.com   melabstractart@gmail.com

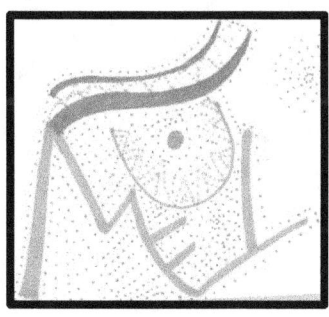

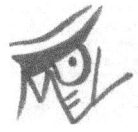

www.ingramcontent.com/pod-product-compliance
Lightning Source LLC
Chambersburg PA
CBHW081451220526
45466CB00008B/2592